Guide to the
Superior Hiking Trail

Linking people with nature by footpath
along Lake Superior's North Shore

D0862169

Superior Hiking Trail Association
Ridgeline Press
2004

Guide to the Superior Hiking Trail

Printed in the United States of America
by McNaughton & Gunn, Inc.
First Edition, 1993
Second Edition, 1998
Third Edition, 2001

Cover and text design: Sally Rauschenfels
Map illustrations: Matt Kania
Cover photo: Jay Steinke
Title page photo: Sam Cook
Illustrations: Dover

*Although the editors and publisher have researched all sources
to ensure the accuracy and completeness of the information
contained in this book, we assume no responsibility for errors,
inaccuracies, omissions or any inconsistency herein.*

ISBN: 0-9636598-3-9

10 9 8 7 6 5 4 3 2

For Tom Peterson and Mark Wester,
the heart and soul of the Superior Hiking Trail

Foreword

What I remember best is squatting on a shoulder of rock, gazing out at the Poplar River Valley. The valley was lush and green and rolled on forever. Down the middle of it meandered the river itself, a reflection of horseshoe bends flowing cool and blue through the lowlands.

I was hot and sweaty from a morning on the trail, and I don't know how long I sat there. I couldn't tell you what I thought about, other than that it was one of the finest places I've ever shed a pack and let the breeze glide over my skin.

Doubtless hundreds of hikers have had the same feeling at a hundred different places along the Superior Hiking Trail.

It is that good.

We owe a large debt to the visionaries who conceived this trail and to Tom Peterson, who must have worn out several pairs of boots choosing its route. It is difficult to hike any distance on the trail without emerging in awe of Peterson's genius and dedication.

And now we have Andrew Slade and a whole crew of other volunteers to thank for this mile-by-mile companion piece to the trail itself. It was a book begging to be written, but which was going to require the spirit of a naturalist and the research of a scientist.

The book's production team, with the help of geologists, botanists, ornithologists, historians and camping experts, has given us a compendium of information about the Superior Hiking Trail. The book's format is hiker-friendly. Its detail is complete. And it fits in a backpack.

This book can help you park your car, arrange a shuttle, find water or find a camp. It'll tell you where you're likely to see a moose or to see Isle Royale, where you're treading in the voyageurs' footsteps and why the rock fractures the way it does along the Split Rock River.

The information in this guide will not weigh you down. It will answer a lot of your questions and free you to get on with the walking.

And maybe one day you'll find yourself doing what I was doing that July morning, what backpacking guru Colin Fletcher calls "sitting on a peak and thinking of nothing at all except perhaps that it is a wonderful thing to sit on a peak and think of nothing at all."

Good reading. Happy walking.

— SAM COOK

The Superior Hiking Trail

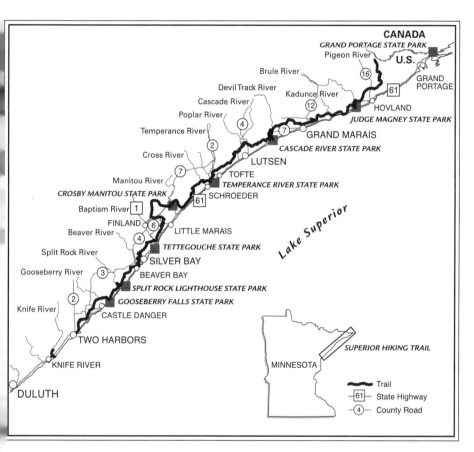

S EE AN EAGLE, FLUSH A GROUSE. Rest in a cool cathedral of pine, shiver atop windswept vistas of Lake Superior. Behold rushing inland rivers, find a moss garden and nap in a field of spring wildflowers. Explore this magnificent landscape shaped by the greatest lake.

Table of Contents

History of the
Superior Hiking Trail

THE SUPERIOR HIKING TRAIL (SHT) WAS conceived in the mid-1980s as a long-distance footpath, modeled after the Appalachian Trail and other long trails, along the ridgeline overlooking Lake Superior's North Shore from Duluth, Minnesota, to the Canadian border. The SHT is complete from Two Harbors on the southwestern end to the Canadian border on the northeastern end. As of April 2004, a through-hike on the trail is 205 miles, and there are 240 miles in the trail system (including overlooks and spur trails).

The Superior Hiking Trail is the realization of an ambitious plan fostered by a group of visionaries—federal, state, and local government employees, artists, resort and business owners, and hiking enthusiasts—who in 1986 incorporated the Superior Hiking Trail Association (SHTA) and made the first request for state funding for trail construction. Three grants from the Legislative Commission on Minnesota Resources (LCMR), each covering a two-year period (1987–89, 1989–91 and 1991–93), were the principal source of funding for early trail construction. The LCMR funds were used primarily to pay the salary of Tom Peterson, the trail construction coordinator "on loan" from the Minnesota Department of Natural Resources, to buy materials, and to finance the crews from the Minnesota Conservation Corps and Lake County that have built substantial portions of the SHT. Other important funding sources have included the U.S. Forest Service, Lake County, and private donations, including corporate contributions.

The SHT was officially opened with a ceremonial "log-cutting" in July 1987, at Britton Peak on the Sawbill Trail, an event attended by federal, state, and local officials and dignitaries, in addition to the Trail's founders. In August 1990, the SHTA sponsored a "Halfway Celebration" at Gooseberry Falls State Park, commemorating the completion of nearly 140 miles of trail—approximately halfway to the goal of a continuous footpath from Duluth to the Canadian border. This celebration was the culmination of the SHTA's first sponsored backpacking trip, in which a dozen hikers trekked the completed Trail in twelve rigorous days. They were greeted by another impressive contingent of dignitaries and well-wishers at Gooseberry Falls State Park.

In September 1991, the Trail was the site of the first "Superior 100" endurance run, in which long-distance "ultra-marathon" runners from around the country competed in a 100-mile race. The race has been run every year since. For a few years in the mid-1990s there was also a snowshoe marathon held on the Trail in the winter.

The first documented through-hiker of the Trail was Paul Hlina in 1995. Paul raised $16,000 in pledges for the SHTA and Wilderness Inquiry as he hiked the length of the trail with crutches due to his paralyzed lower extremities.

Though a relative newcomer to the country's long-distance trails, and a toddler by comparison with its prototype and model, the Appalachian Trail (conceived in 1921 and completed, in its first layout, fifteen years later), the SHT has already won national recognition. It has been featured in countless regional publications and broadcasts and has been the subject of stories in national magazines, such as *Prevention, Walking* and *Backpacker* magazines. *Prevention* identified the Superior Hiking Trail as one of the twelve best trails in the national forests, and *Backpacker* Magazine rated it one of the ten best in the country.

Some changes are on the horizon for the Superior Hiking Trail. It is slated to become part of the North Country National Scenic Trail, a 4,500-mile footpath stretching from New York to North Dakota. The Superior Hiking Trail will retain its own identity and will still be maintained and managed by SHTA, but it will also be a segment of this national trail.

With becoming a part of the North Country Trail, SHTA amended its mission to build the SHT to the southwest from Two Harbors through Duluth, Jay Cooke State Park, and on to the Wisconsin border, another 80 miles of trail. Plans are being made to lay out these future sections of trail and hopefully this addition will be accomplished in the next decade.

General Description of the Trail

THE SUPERIOR HIKING TRAIL IS DESIGNED AS A footpath only, comprised mainly of an 18-inch treadway through a clearing approximately four feet in width. SHTA policy prohibits the use of motorized vehicles, mountain bikes and horses on the Trail. The steepness and narrowness of the SHT in most areas make it unsuitable for cross-country skiing, although snowshoe travel is possible.

For most of its length, the SHT is routed along the ridgeline overlooking Lake Superior. At its lowest point, the SHT goes along the lakeshore, which is 602 feet above sea level. At its highest point, in the hills of the Jackson Lake area, the SHT is 1,829 feet above sea level and more than 1,200 feet above Lake Superior. The SHT is characterized by ascents to rock outcroppings and cliffs, and descents into numerous river and creek valleys crossed by attractive and functional bridges. The SHT traverses a rich variety of terrain and habitat types. Woodlands of birch and aspen give way to stands of pine, fir and lush cedar groves. Grassy clearings, products of lumbering operations and forest fires, provide interesting variation from the more prevalent woodland scenes. Panoramic overlooks of Lake Superior, the Sawtooth Mountains and inland woodlands, lakes, and rivers are abundant along the length of the SHT. At many points, the SHT follows rivers and creeks, often for distances of a mile or more, showcasing waterfalls and rapids, bends and deep gorges where rushing water over thousands of years has cut into layers of ancient volcanic bedrock. Steep portions of the SHT are accessed by log and stone stairways handcrafted by trail crews.

Hikers enjoy varied forest scenes. The gradual transition from oak, maple and basswood to the boreal forest of balsam, pine, spruce, cedar, and tamarack is interrupted by regrowth forest of aspen and birch. Wildlife abounds: encounters with deer are common, as well as sightings of moose, beaver, black bear, eagles and grouse. Fortunate hikers will remember many varieties of songbirds. Wildflowers are especially prevalent in the spring, but some varieties are evident through the hiking season. Wild blueberries and raspberries provide a special midsummer treat at many points along the SHT.

The SHT crosses national forest and state park lands, state and county property, and private property. The SHT reaches the Canadian border where the Swamp River meets the Pigeon River, and along its route connects and traverses seven state parks. Many property owners— individuals and corporations, in addition to governmental units—have granted easements or permissions for the SHT to cross their land. In some areas, special restrictions apply as conditions of the permissions that have been granted on private lands. Please observe and obey all posted restrictions (such as requirements to stay on the trail through private property, or prohibitions on fires, camping or hunting). The privilege to use these private lands depends upon the cooperation of Trail users and their respect for the special restrictions.

The one constant feature of the SHT, and the characteristic that distinguishes it from other forest trails, is the presence of Lake Superior—the legendary lake Native Americans celebrated in song and story as "Gitche Gumme." Although the distance to the big lake varies considerably along the SHT, its presence is always felt. Sometimes the "lake effect" weather brings cool breezes and moisture in to shore, though in summer it may be 20 degrees warmer just over the ridge. The SHT features many spectacular views of Lake Superior, as well as many more subtle views through the trees, allowing the hiker an endless selection of spots to rest, lunch and meditate against the backdrop of the lake's many moods and colors. From some vantage points, the Wisconsin/Michigan shoreline is visible on the horizon; other views feature islands—Isle Royale on the northern part of the SHT, and the Apostles on the southern end.

Lake Superior itself is 31,280 square miles—the largest freshwater lake in the world by area. It is 350 miles long and 160 miles wide at its farthest dimensions. Its average depth is 489 feet, and its maximum depth is 1,333 feet. As a part of the Great Lakes shipping corridor, it is the inland terminus of a commercial shipping trade that reaches to the East Coast and across the Atlantic Ocean. After the ice departs in spring, until sometime in January, the hiker can spot big vessels on the lake—the ore and grain freighters that carry midwestern exports to points east, and the "salties" that come from ports across the ocean. In the summer months when the lake is more often placid than angry, hikers can see sailboats, charter fishing boats and even small motorboats, canoes, and kayaks near the shore. Lake Superior's shipwrecks are legendary and are documented at places such as the Split Rock Lighthouse visitor center and in books and paintings found in the many galleries and shops along the North Shore. Lake Superior, with its history and its beauty, gives the SHT a unique and unforgettable character.

ACCESSING AND USING THE TRAIL

The SHT is accessible directly from Minnesota Highway 61, on spur trails accessed from 61, or on many intersecting roads. Seven of the state parks along the North Shore (including Crosby-Manitou State Park, which is inland) are connected by the SHT and provide access to it. Along Highway 61, look for the brown signs with the Superior Hiking Trail logo on them. The distance between access points—most from five to ten miles apart—makes the SHT easily divisible into one-way day-hikes, accomplished by leaving a vehicle at the access point destination and shuttling to the next access point to begin the hike. If your party does not have two vehicles, you can use the Superior Shuttle service (at (218) 834-5511 or www.superiorshuttle.com) or possibly local resorts or outfitters. Numerous other possibilities exist for day hikes and loop hikes, some employing state park or national forest trails. Of course, a hike to a point on the trail with a return along the same trail is never a disappointment. The vista you missed over your shoulder on the way in is revealed in all its splendor on the way out. Rewarding day hikes are spotlighted in this book in the chapter, "Best of the Superior Hiking Trail," on page 42.

When planning a hike, allow one hour for every one-and-a-half to two miles. Day-hikers should carry a pack with adequate water (river and lake water along the SHT must be treated before it is consumed), snacks, sunscreen, bug repellent, toilet paper, compass, flashlight, and an extra clothing layer and raingear if conditions warrant. Remember that weather conditions can change rapidly; dark storm clouds and chilly winds sometimes move in quickly and unexpectedly on what began as a warm, cloudless day. If you plan to hike more than one or two hours, it is best to be prepared for weather changes.

You should always carry a map when you are on the trail. There are places where the SHT crosses other trails and roads, or times when the trail is covered with leaves or snow, that may be confusing. SHTA publishes and sells several types of maps for the trail. State park visitor centers and stores on the North Shore also sell the maps.

Dogs must be on a leash at all times. Remember, even though your dog may be friendly, there may be people hiking on the trail who are afraid of dogs. Also, no pack animals are allowed on the trail.

Each season of the year offers its own rewards for the SHT hiker. Spring is a time for wildflowers, bird songs, and the unique color of emerging leaves. Summer brings the long hiking days and the sort of heat that makes a dip in one of the cool rivers all the more inviting. Fall is a symphony of colors and smells on the SHT, and the lack of biting insects makes it the friendliest time of year to hike. Fall also brings deer hunting season. Many sections of the SHT are closed during deer season. Check with the Superior Hiking Trail office or check the website for a list of closures. Signs are posted at trailheads to advise of trail closings. If you do hike on sections that are not posted closed, be sure to wear blaze orange clothing and stay alert.

Winter is a time of quiet magic on the SHT. While cross-country skiing would be nearly impossible, snowshoeing is increasingly popular. The SHTA offers group snowshoe hikes each winter. The primary differences between winter and non-winter use of the SHT are that snowshoeing takes much longer than hiking and some of the parking lots are not plowed.

The SHT is also ideally suited for long-distance hiking. The hiker seeking an extended trip can hike the 205 miles of the SHT to its northeastern end, then continue along the Border Route Trail, which in turn links with the Kekekabic Trail. These connections provide a multi-week adventure of over 300 miles, from near Ely in the west to near Grand

Portage in the east, and then southwestward to Two Harbors on the Superior Hiking Trail.

There are 81 backcountry campsites provided along the SHT. Each campsite has 2-8 tent pads, a fire ring, and a backcountry latrine. There are no reservations, fees, or permits required to use these campsites. Parties are required to share campsites if tent pads are available. Since the trail crosses so much private land and state park land and often these land ownerships are not marked, campers must camp only at the designated campsites.

For additional information about backpacking on the SHT and tips for overnight trips, see the "Backpacking Primer" chapter on page 33.

For the long-distance hiker who prefers more amenities, lodge-to-lodge hiking is available. You need carry only a daypack, since lodge staff help you shuttle to your next trail destination each day. For more information on lodge-to-lodge hiking, contact Boundary Country Trekking toll-free at (800) 322-8327 or at www.boundarycountry.com.

This guidebook is designed to be a functional resource for you to plan your hiking adventure on the Superior Hiking Trail. The text is broken into segments, with a description of each trail section, and information on parking, access points and campsites. In addition, the highlights of each segment are featured—rivers, waterfalls, overlooks and other natural features. To enhance your hiking experience, information on human and natural history, both fact and legend, are also included, as well as explanations for some of the natural phenomena observed. This information will maximize your enjoyment of the SHT.

Geology and Scenery along the North Shore

MINNESOTA'S SHORELANDS OF LAKE SUPERIOR—the "North Shore"—is a land of rugged, forested hills, sweeping vistas of blue, green, autumn red and gold, and winter white, rocky headlands and crashing waves, cozy valleys and surging waterfalls. The dramatically beautiful landscape that we see today is a consequence of a geological history that goes back more than a billion years, into Late Precambrian time.

Regional geologic studies have shown that what is now the upper Great Lakes area had undergone several major periods of volcanism, intense deformation of the earth's crust, sedimentation and mountain-building. By about 1.2 billion years ago, erosion had eventually reduced the area to a low, rolling plain. There were no Great Lakes.

Then about 1.1 billion years ago the center of North America began to split apart as slow upwellings in the earth's hot, stiff-plastic mantle (beneath the crust) began to melt, and huge volumes of molten rock (magma) leaked up to the surface along fissures in the crust. The present remains of this world-scale crustal feature, known as the Midcontinent Rift System, extend from southeastern Michigan north under the lower peninsula, westward through Lake Superior, and south-southwest beneath the Twin Cities and Iowa to northeast Kansas. Most of the magma was erupted as great, pancake-like flows of "flood basalt," of a composition similar to the modern or recent eruptions on Hawaii,

Iceland or the Snake River Plain in Idaho. Hundreds of individual lava flows erupted, building up a sequence of layers up to five miles thick along the North Shore area and even thicker along the axis of the rift, now under Lake Superior.

As the crust was pulled apart, stretched and thinned, and magma erupted onto the surface from the mantle beneath, the center of the rift gradually subsided, leaving the rock layers tilted on the flanks towards the rift axis. Erosion during the last billion years has etched out these tilted layers to form the "Sawtooth Mountains." These are a series of long ridges with a relatively gentle southeast slope toward Lake Superior and a steep northwest slope, each one sculpted from a single huge lava flow.

Some basaltic magma never made it to the surface, but squeezed between older layers and solidified at various levels in the crust. When magma cools and crystallizes slowly it tends to produce larger crystals and the rocks thus formed (intrusive rocks) are generally more resistant when eventually exposed to erosion at the Earth's surface. A very large complex of intrusions, the Duluth Complex, underlies prominent highlands stretching from downtown Duluth southwestward past Spirit Mountain to Bardon Peak, and overlooks the St. Louis River valley and Wisconsin. (This same Duluth Complex also extends inland northward almost to Ely and eastward into Cook County.)

Smaller intrusions, mainly the dark rock diabase, squeezed in at higher levels within the lava-flow sequence. Some of these make up such prominent hills along the North Shore as Hawk Ridge at Duluth, Silver Cliff, most of the rugged highlands between Beaver Bay and Little Marais, Leveaux and Oberg Mountains and the ski hills at Lutsen. Diabase hills continue in the Hovland area and beyond Grand Portage, with the great ramparts of Hat Point, Mt. Josephine and the ridge beyond that overlooks Wauswaugoning Bay.

In some places these diabase magmas carried up huge blocks of a whitish rock called anorthosite, torn loose from the base of the crust about 25 miles beneath the surface. These anorthosites are very resistant to erosion, and now "hold up" such landmarks as Split Rock Lighthouse, Mt. Trudee and other knobs in Tettegouche State Park, and the greatest of all, Carlton Peak at Tofte.

The great volumes of hot magma that worked their way up through the older crust melted some of it. This new magma had the composition of rhyolite or granite, with more silica and less iron than the basaltic magmas, and when it solidified it formed light-colored rocks in contrast to the dark basalt and diabase. Several very large rhyolite flows erupted; one of them forms the magnificent features of Palisade Head and Shovel Point in Lake County. Big rhyolites have also been eroded to form the deep gorges of the Devil Track, Kadunce, and Brule Rivers in Cook County, and of Split Rock River in Lake County.

For some as yet unknown reason, rifting and volcanism ended fairly abruptly without the continent coming completely apart to form a new ocean basin. The last major volcanic sequence can now be seen as the "backbone" of Isle Royale and of Keweenaw Point, far across Lake Superior in Michigan. The rift continued to sink for awhile, however, and streams washed sand, pebbles and mud into the slowly subsiding basin. Several miles of such sediment accumulated in the middle, some of which can be seen today on the Bayfield Peninsula and Apostle Islands, Wisconsin, as well as on southern Isle Royale. Finally, over a period of perhaps 100 million years, the crust stabilized, and the buried sediments gradually hardened into rock. The most dramatic episode in Lake Superior history was over, and erosion by streams took over. But there was still no Lake Superior.

The last chapter in the saga of the North Shore's landscape is the Great Ice Age. Several times during the last two million years (most recently only about 14,000 years ago) great continental glaciers, up to one or two miles thick, built up and oozed southward from Canada. The great ice streams were mainly eroding the underlying rock, some of which had become deeply weathered. Moving southwestward, the Superior Lobe of the ice sheet carried debris (including volcanic rocks, agates and sandstone) from the North Shore area as far as the Twin Cities, the Minnesota River Valley, and even to Iowa. The ice found the sedimentary rocks in the middle of the old Midcontinent Rift System to be relatively easy to erode, and it excavated what was to be the Lake Superior basin well below sea level. As the glacier melted back about 11,000 years ago, it uncovered this great scooped-out depression that of course filled with water. Early stages (such as Glacial Lake Duluth) were several hundred feet higher than the present Lake Superior, because the ice was still blocking the outlet. Look for rounded beach stones along the trail, high above the current lake level. About 5,000 years ago, Lake Superior as we know it today was well established. Since glaciation, the forests have covered the land, the North Shore rivers have been eroding their gorges, and waves have been making beaches and eating away at the shore cliffs and bluffs.

As you hike the SHT, remember this geologic history that has shaped the landscape. Look for evidence of volcanic activity, the "squeezed in" intrusions, glacial erosion and deposition, abandoned beaches far above the present l3ake level and on-going geologic processes. Enjoy the geologic dimension!

Habitats of the Superior Hiking Trail

THE SUPERIOR HIKING TRAIL FOLLOWS A corridor that is long enough to have members of three general vegetational groups along its length. One of these is the northern hardwood forest that is at the northwestern limit of its distribution. These northern hardwoods, such as sugar maple, basswood, and oak, are concentrated in the highlands that form the setting for so much of the SHT. This group becomes less common as one travels northeastward from Duluth, and some species disappear completely by Cook County. The second group includes boreal species, like paper birch, balsam fir, and white spruce, which range across northern Minnesota. As the northern hardwoods thin out to the northeast, this second group becomes more prevalent along the SHT. The third group, the Great Lakes St. Lawrence forest, consists of species found primarily to the east from the Great Lakes to the St. Lawrence lowland but not ranging far to the north or south. The eastern white pine exemplifies this forest group.

Members of each of these forest groups exist side-by-side in a wide variety of different plant communities. By understanding where a tree comes from geographically, you can begin to make sense of why it is found in particular parts of the SHT. For example, you will find white spruce often in dark, cool valleys that better resemble northern habitat than the warmer, drier ridgetops. Glaciers deposited the rare deep soil along some of the ridges, providing a soil and a habitat for maples quite similar to that found in states further to the south.

THE NORTHERN HARDWOOD GROUP

Sugar maple is typically the most common tree in the northern hardwoods. Like many others in this group, it is associated with upper slopes, which are less frosty in the late spring. Sugar maple stands occur in all segments of the SHT. They were tapped for sugar by the Ojibway people. Sugar maple forests make fall hikes on the SHT glorious, turning hillsides into gold and red. Sugar maples can be identified by their leaves, whose well-known shape is seen on the Canadian flag.

Northern red oak is another northern hardwood. It is a large tree at the southwest end of the SHT. However, at the end of its range near the Lake/Cook County line, the oak is a small tree on rocky knobs. Its deep maroon leaves are among the last to drop in the fall.

Yellow birch can grow to the greatest diameter of any of the northern hardwoods. It may be identified in all seasons by scraping the bark from a twig and sniffing for the distinctive odor of wintergreen. These trees sometimes begin life on a dead log, which later rots away to leave a yellow birch growing "on stilts." This species often develops a hollow trunk, and so is an important site for animal denning or nesting.

Other less common members of this group include basswood, ironwood (hop hornbeam) and American elm.

THE BOREAL FOREST GROUP

Paper birch is extremely common throughout all but wet ground along the SHT. Its white bark and black twigs are more distinctive than its rather plain leaves. This tree requires sunny conditions for growth and fades from the scene as forest stands age and shade the forest floor. Droughts in the late 1980's have led to an extensive dieback of this species, especially near roads and clearcuts.

Balsam fir is a common tree in all parts of the SHT corridor. It seldom achieves great age or size before a storm knocks it down or spruce budworm kills it. Its needles are "flat and friendly," which distinguishes it from the "spiky" spruce. Crushing these needles will bring out an aroma reminiscent of winter holidays.

White spruce thrives throughout the SHT corridor where soils are deep enough. You can roll its needles between two fingers, and its bark is rougher than the balsam fir's bark. Large individuals are found here and there. On rock outcrops or in bogs, you may see black spruce, a smaller species. Black spruce is otherwise uncommon because of the scarcity of bogs near Lake Superior.

Balsam poplar is found predominantly in wet soil near streams. The long, sticky aromatic buds are distinctive and perfume the woods during leaf-out in the spring.

Jack pine is scarce along the North Shore in general. The damp summer and lack of expanses of coarse or shallow soils curtail the frequency of the fires on which this species depends.

THE GREAT LAKES/ST. LAWRENCE GROUP

Several species have their ranges centered in the Great Lakes-St. Lawrence River lowland to the east of Lake Superior. They overlap about equally with the northern portion of the hardwoods and the southern portion of the boreal forest.

Among these species is white pine. White pine is a distinctively majestic tree, with its feathery branches and dark trunk. On closer examination, you'll find that the needles come in clumps of five, as opposed to clumps of two with the red pine. This species was abundant over much of the North Shore region prior to logging. If you see a large, rotting stump on your hike, it is likely the remnant of a white pine that fell to the lumberjacks. The North Shore has a climate that is extremely favorable for the white pine blister rust fungus, so efforts to replant this species have been less successful here than in many other former pineries.

White cedar is common on both wet streams and dry rock outcrops, but only occasional on deep, well-drained soils. What these seemingly contradictory habitats have in common is a lower frequency of fire. White cedar, wherever you find it, is an important winter food for deer. You can identify this tree by its broad, flat, scaly needles and its stringy bark.

OTHER TREES

Red pine grows in scattered groves, often associated with rock outcrops. Like white pine, it was more abundant before the logging era, though not as common as its five-needled cousin. Disease does not currently pose a great threat to this species, which is also known as "Norway pine" and is the state tree of Minnesota.

Black ash is found mostly in damp ground, rarely with hardwoods on the uplands. It is abundant near many streams. This species seems to be the ultimate in caution, as it is the last to leaf out and the first to drop its leaves.

Heartleaf birch is a little-known tree that barely enters the North Shore from the east. It resembles paper birch but has a rosy tinge to its bark. Also, it tends to have branches farther down the trunk than does paper birch, as heartleaf birch is more tolerant of shade. Despite the name, leaf shape is not easy to use for identification. In fact, some botanists list this as a variety of paper birch.

Quaking aspen, also known as "popple" or "poplar," fits into all of the above groups and is one of the most common trees on the SHT. This species occupies more territory than any other North American tree, being found well to the north, south, east and west (with a hiatus in the Great Plains). It can be expected in the trail corridor wherever there are younger forests on deep soils. Old, shady stands are unlikely to have much aspen, although large trembling aspen are found in some places. This species increased greatly as the land was opened up by lumbering for pine and by the fires that sometimes followed.

PLANTS

This diversity of tree types parallels a diversity of wildflowers and other herbaceous growth. Minor variations in soil types can lead to major changes in the flora on the forest floor. Some stretches of rich soil will be covered with large-leaf aster and bluebead lily, while bare granitic rock may support some caribou moss and the polypody fern. Each month of spring, summer, and fall brings a new range of color and growth. As the snow melts in spring, look for violets, marsh marigold and wild lily-of-the-valley. As summer nears, the moccasin flowers and ladyslippers bloom, often in isolated and hard-to-find patches. In the heat of summer, watch for columbine, wild roses, buttercup and the towering cow parsnip. The onset of fall brings the asters and the goldenrods, which can bloom well into October. There is a useful chart on page 110.

Other flowers grow in distinct habitats, such as the water lilies and cattails in marshes, labrador tea and bog laurel in bogs, and twinflower, wintergreen and indian pipe in pine duff.

Overall, let these clues of trees and flowers guide you to an understanding of the varied terrain through which the SHT passes. On any given section of the trail you will pass through three, four or a dozen different habitats. Landforms, microclimates and succession determined these habitats, and the trees and other plants tell you fascinating stories about survival, and thriving, in the north woods.

Birds of the
Lake Superior Highlands

O NE OF THE GREAT PLEASURES IN WALKING through the woods is being attuned to what other creatures are inhabiting the same piece of ground. Most forest animals are wary (at least those higher taxonomically than insects!), and their presence is not easily revealed. Birds, because they fly and they sing while nesting, are more conspicuous than most other vertebrates and thus add a dimension to the hike, whether you are teasing out a scolding ovenbird from the undergrowth or watching hawks migrate in the fall from one of the many overlooks.

The type of birdwatching you may experience along the Superior Hiking Trail depends on the character of the woods, the season of the year and the weather. Dedicated bird watchers with a penchant for listing notable species travel to the North Shore in search of gulls, sea ducks, and out-of-range migrants accidently appearing on the shore of Lake Superior. This search can be exciting sport, but an equally rewarding experience can be found in discovering what birds inhabit the forest that covers the hills back from shore. Now that the SHT provides good access to these woods, one can hike, look and listen for some of the approximately 100 species of birds that breed in the Lake Superior Highlands in summer. During both spring and fall migration, congregations of woodland birds are occasionally encountered, but the winter woods are virtually silent since most of the birds have gone to more southerly wintering grounds.

BIRDS OF PONDS AND STREAMS

- great blue heron
- wood duck
- mallard
- blue-winged teal
- ring-necked duck
- common goldeneye
- hooded merganser
- spotted sandpiper
- belted kingfisher
- tree swallow

BIRDS OF LOWLAND CONIFERS

- olive-sided flycatcher
- yellow-bellied flycatcher
- gray jay
- boreal chickadee
- Connecticut warbler
- Lincoln's sparrow

Lake Superior Highlands describes the ecoregion that the Superior Hiking Trail traverses. Ecoregions are defined by topography, climate, soils and vegetation. Habitat for birds is almost entirely determined by the vegetation, which on the forested hills of the Lake Superior Highlands is a mixture of deciduous and coniferous types with hardwood forest types predominant. Openings, either woodland ponds and streams, brushlands or cutovers, provide variety, as does an occasional boreal conifer bog or open ledge. These unusual habitats provide opportunities to see some rare nesting species.

Four species of raptors—turkey vulture, osprey, bald eagle, and peregrine falcon—might be spotted flying over the forest from a rocky knob or pond edge. Two other species—red-tailed hawk and American kestrel—could be encountered nesting in forest that has been broken up by logging or other clearings. The deep-woods hawks—sharp-shinned, goshawk and broad-winged—are more numerous but rarely seen. The best evidence of their presence is the alarm cries given near a nesting site. Merlins are also very vociferous near the nest but are mostly found around big conifers along lakeshores.

Woodland ponds provide a place to see ducks, especially those that nest in tree cavities. A small colony of great blue herons or tree swallows might be discovered in a beaver pond, and spotted sandpipers can be found bobbing along the rocks of open streams.

Where boreal conifer lowlands intersect the upland forest, a number of species confined to that special habitat can be located. Some of them, because they are rare breeders on a national scale, are much sought after by birders. Pockets of shrubby wetlands or water edges provide habitat for another group of species not otherwise present in the forested hills.

The greatest portion of the species present along the SHT, about three-fourths, are upland forest inhabitants, most of which are only there for a short period of time during the breeding season (early May to early August). At least 73 species probably nest in these uplands, including the three hawks mentioned before, four owls (great horned, barred, long-eared, saw-whet), five other non-passerines (ruffed grouse, black-billed cuckoo, whip-poor-will, chimney swift, ruby-throated hummingbird), five wood-peckers, and 56 passerines (songbirds).

A very few of these birds are permanent residents and might be found in winter woods on a snowshoe trek. The rest are here in the summer to take advantage of the abundant insects (mostly caterpillars) to feed their young and the many diverse habitats provided by the mixed forest, including its cut-over patches and natural shrubby openings.

The diversity of the upland forest is the key to the richness of nesting species found there. Although most of the contiguous forest is deciduous, it is mixed with varying amounts of conifers, which sometimes form fairly pure stands. The age of the forest also varies from young, shrubby stands to big, old trees that form a dense canopy. Each habitat type has certain species that are adapted to what it provides for food and shelter, but some species are more specialized in their requirements than others. Those that are mostly restricted to wetlands and openings have already been

BIRDS OF SHRUB WETLANDS

- American woodcock
- alder flycatcher
- gray catbird
- golden-winged warbler
- Tennessee warbler
- yellow warbler
- northern waterthrush
- common yellowthroat
- Wilson's warbler
- swamp sparrow

PERMANENT RESIDENTS

- goshawk
- ruffed grouse
- spruce grouse
- great horned owl
- barred owl
- downy woodpecker
- hairy woodpecker
- pileated woodpecker
- blue jay
- common raven
- black-capped chickadee
- red-breasted nuthatch

MOST COMMON UPLAND BIRDS

- least flycatcher
- red-eyed vireo
- veery
- American robin
- Nashville warbler
- chestnut-sided warbler
- magnolia warbler
- yellow-rumped warbler
- black-throated green warbler
- blackburnian warbler
- black-and-white warbler
- American redstart
- ovenbird
- mourning warbler
- Canada warbler
- rose-breasted grosbeak
- chipping sparrow
- song sparrow
- white-throated sparrow

mentioned; and since these habitats are rare along the SHT, so are these species.

There are 73 species that are considered upland, forest-dependent breeding birds. The raptors (hawks and owls) have already been listed. They have large territories and their population density is quite low, so spotting one is a thrill. Most of the other forest nesting birds are more abundant, but small songbirds are not easily noticed in the thick vegetation. About half of the woodland birds belong to just four taxonomic families: thrushes (5 species), vireos (4 species), warblers (17 species) and sparrows/finches (11 species).

The summer hiker who is not a birder is probably amazed that the woods contain so many species. Except for the dawn chorus (starting from 4:30 a.m. when even a dedicated nature explorer is likely asleep), their presence is only revealed by scolding chips or an occasional burst of song. To really appreciate the birds along the SHT, learning the songs, at least of some of the common species, will add immense pleasure to the hiking experience. The intense singing period is at the height of the nesting cycle, which is a very short time from early June to early July.

There are some good, commercial birding tapes that aid in learning bird songs, but the best way is spotting the songster with binoculars and identifying it while it sings.

Two species are much prized by birders because the North Shore forest is the only place in Minnesota that they are known to regularly breed: Philadelphia vireo and black-throated blue warbler.

Weather is always a variable in bird-watching, and windy days slow down song and other bird activity considerably. However, in the fall it is on those glorious days with a good northwest wind, following the passage of a cold front, that hawk-watching is the most rewarding. Hawks and other day-time migrants are funneled along the shore of Lake Superior and use the updrafts from the hills to aid them in their flight. The bulk of the hawk migration is from about the 10th of September through the 10th of October, but eagles and northern raptors can be seen on days with good migration weather through early December.

The overlooks along the SHT provide opportunities for witnessing this migration, although concentrations are not nearly as large as near Duluth. Other birds migrate in flocks, usually in the morning, and can be seen in numbers in a wide band along the North Shore in the fall: blue jay, American crow, common raven, American robin, cedar waxwing and seven species of winter finches.

In both spring (May) and fall (September through early October), flocks of small birds can be encountered, usually spotted feeding intensely in the treetops (vireos and warblers) or flushed while walking along the trail (thrushes and sparrows). Their presence depends on the weather they have encountered during migration. Local breeding birds also congregate in foraging flocks after the nesting season and before they set out on their long-distance migration to the tropics. They are often joined by the permanent residents, chickadees and woodpeckers, who usually announce their presence by their flocking calls.

Each hiking trip, depending on time and place, can produce a different experience with the birds in the woods. Storing up these moments expands the memory of the event and can also add to the knowledge of the birds of the Lake Superior Highlands.

Animals of the
Superior Hiking Trail

DESCRIBING THE ANIMAL LIFE OF THE North Shore and the Superior Hiking Trail is challenging because of its great variety. Fortunately, for the sake of brevity, it's possible to make some distinctions. First of all, there are animals in the official sense, that is, things that move and eat other things. But then there are "animals," generally fuzzy things with one set of eyes. Is that black fly biting your earlobe an animal? Yes, indeed. But a lot of people would rather swat the black fly while looking for a "real" animal like a deer, wolf, or turtle. Insects, reptiles, fish, and amphibians are all animals but, due to space, will receive only short notice here. And the birds of the Superior Hiking Trail are covered in the previous chapter. This chapter will mostly cover the mammals of the SHT.

As you hike, you may encounter animals of three basic types:

1) Small animals that are common but seldom seen;

2) Medium-size animals that are somewhat common and often seen; and

3) Medium to large, generally carnivorous animals that are rare, wide-ranging and also seldom seen.

On your typical day hike you probably won't see a lot of animals besides birds and insects. That's not because they aren't there. But unless you have the eyes of a hawk, you'll likely miss the mice and shrews that cruise the underbrush. And unless you are quiet and lucky, you probably won't see a wolf. However, white-tail deer, snowshoe hare and red squirrel, among others, are animals that are commonly seen along the SHT.

Although you may not see any large mammal, you will undoubtedly see some evidence of their passing. They are out there. Many mammals are active during the morning and evenings, but rest during the day. The white-tail deer you see bounding through the forest may have been resting from a busy night of feeding before you startled it. If you want to learn about the animals of the SHT, you will do better to look for evidence rather than the animal itself.

If you do look for animal signs, you won't be disappointed. In a muddy section of the SHT, look for tracks of deer, moose and wolves, animals likely to use the SHT as an easy path through remote woods. Scat (animal feces) is another obvious sign, and it becomes more obvious when an animal uses scat to mark territory. When there is a prominent, bare rock near the trail, look for wolf or coyote scat (told by the ropy texture, hair and bone chip content) or that of the fisher or marten (which is long, slender, and dark). All these mammals use scat to mark their territory with both its sight and smell. Other signs of large animals include bark rubbings by male moose and deer, deer and moose beds in grassy areas, and nests. If this sort of animal watching interests you, bring a book such as Peterson's *A Field Guide to Animal Tracks*. There are some fascinating stories to be read in the woods.

SMALL ANIMALS THAT ARE COMMON BUT SELDOM SEEN

This category includes all the shrews, voles, mice, and little weasels. These animals are used to fleeing at the sound (or feel) of danger. You'll see their trails crossing above or sometimes below the SHT. In open areas, look for the birds like kestrels that are looking, in turn, for these little creatures. At dusk, in a campsite, a woodland deer mouse or short-tailed shrew might try to get into your food or clean up your dinner scraps.

These small creatures play important roles in ecosystems as primary consumers and carnivores (mostly of insects). They also aerate and enrich the soil with their tunnels. For every one large, dramatic carnivore in the food web there are thousands of little creatures, all doing their part to keep the cycles flowing. And in case you are fortunate enough to encounter one, remember that the short-tailed shrew is one of only two North American mammals with a venomous bite.

MEDIUM-TO-LARGE SIZE ANIMALS THAT ARE SOMEWHAT COMMON AND OFTEN SEEN

White-tail deer. Although the deer is a common resident now, a century ago there were hardly any here. Instead there were woodland caribou, which thrived on lichens and moss of the primordial forest. Now, with logging and other habitat changes, the caribou are only in Canada (with the notable exception of a caribou wandering in Hovland in the winter of 1980-81). Deer congregate along the North Shore in winter and early spring, where snowfall is lighter and melts sooner, making food more accessible and travel easier. The Jonvik deer yard near Lutsen is one of the largest deer yards in the state. For two weeks in the fall, generally the first and second weeks in November, deer are hunted all along the Superior Hiking Trail, so wear bright colors.

Moose. Count yourself fortunate if you encounter one of these gentle giants on your hike. You'll increase your luck if you look carefully in the low, wet areas near the SHT. Look for a brown boulder moving among the lily pads. In general, deer and moose populations do not intermix. The deer carry a flatworm that doesn't harm the deer but is fatal to the moose. Moose droppings are thumb-size, light brown pellets, found in large piles. Moose tracks have the same double half-moon shape of the deer, but are at least twice as long. Some classic moose habitat along the Superior Hiking Trail includes Jonvik Creek and the wetlands around Grand Portage.

Black bear. The black bear is an incredible survivor. It uses every trick in the book to survive the north woods. Bears have one of the most diverse natural diets around, including your food bag if you're not careful. Bears' diet follows the season: when the blueberries are ripe, they gorge on blueberries, and likewise with the hazelnuts or other edibles. When there's no more fresh food, around the end of September, bears begin to go into torpor, a sort of intermittent hibernation. The SHT passes near a grove of oak trees in Tettegouche State Park that is a magnet for bears from 50 miles around when the acorns are ripe in the fall. Treat these creatures with the respect they deserve—that includes putting your food far out of reach when you're camping.

Weasels. You may not see a weasel, but weasels are mammals worth noting. There is a whole family of weasels of all different sizes, all with the same mode of survival: chase and kill. The short-tailed weasel, or ermine, chases mice; the fisher and marten chase larger prey such as squirrels and hares. You'll be thrilled if you ever witness one of their chases. In the winter, look for their distinctive bounding tracks in the snow.

Snowshoe hare. Depending on their population cycles, you may see lots of hares or you may see none. Even if they are around, you have to look carefully. With their changing coat, they are always well camouflaged. They prefer thickets of shrubs and short trees, which give them plenty of cover from predators such as great-horned owls and lynx.

Red squirrel. The sound of a red squirrel defending its territory is one of the standard anthems of the north woods. That sharp, rattling "chirrrr" is the squirrel's way of telling you to beat it. Each squirrel defends a territory of about a 200-yard diameter circle. If the summer and fall harvests are good, the squirrel will store up to 14,000 food items in this territory, including cones, mushrooms and nuts (the mushrooms are hung on tree bark where they can dry). Red squirrels can become overly friendly in campsites if they are fed by hikers.

Beaver. As the SHT works its way up and down hills and across streams, it is bound to take you through the work of the beaver. Sometimes, though, you won't even notice. The beaver, with its propensity to change the environment to suit its needs (like another mammal, *Homo sapiens*), has been around long enough that its ponds have turned into forests. Some particularly spectacular beaver ponds can be found near Sawmill Creek and on Jonvik Creek, where the SHT crosses the creek on a beaver dam, as well as along the upper reaches of the Gooseberry River.

MEDIUM-TO-LARGE, GENERALLY CARNIVOROUS ANIMALS THAT ARE RARE, WIDE-RANGING AND ALSO SELDOM SEEN

Timber wolf. Along the North Shore, starting northeast of Two Harbors, there are numerous packs of wolves. This is, however, the fringe of their population. The traffic and development of Highway 61 keeps most wolves inland, though the Superior Hiking Trail leads through some prime wolf territory. To see a wolf you would have to know its travel paths and disguise yourself from sight or smell. Look for scat and tracks along the SHT, and also the occasional kill site of a well-broken-up deer carcass. The presence of the wolves is a testimony to the wildness of the land through which you are traveling.

Coyote. Where there aren't wolves along the North Shore, there are likely to be coyotes. Wolves defend their territories from coyotes, but as the edge of wolf range fluctuates, so does the coyote range. Coyotes are smaller than wolves but larger than foxes and can be identified by their large ears and bouncing gait. They're more of a "suburban" animal, more accustomed to human presence. Like wolves, they have eerie, though distinct, howling sessions.

Lynx, Bobcat, and Mountain Lion. Solitary hunters, these wild cats prey mostly on the snowshoe hare, and so their populations vary with the hare's. The bobcat is at the northern edge of its range and the lynx is at its southern edge. The lynx travels 3–6 miles a night in search of food, but success is less than fifty-fifty each night. Both cats have ranges rather than territories, which means they can overlap with others of the same species and are not generally defended. Another even bigger cat, the mountain lion, has been spotted in recent years in St. Louis and Cook Counties.

OTHER ANIMALS ON THE SUPERIOR HIKING TRAIL

Insects are animals, right? If you're out in May through September, you'll likely encounter some of these. Not all of them are out to bite you, either. But some will try. Watch for black flies in May and June, various species of mosquito from May to September, and deer and horse flies in July and August. Look for dragonflies, leeches, colorful beetles, and aquatic insects in the streams. Also in the streams you'll find brook trout, and a host of frogs, turtles, and salamanders.

The animal life along the North Shore is a significant part of what makes the SHT so special. With careful observation, you'll find that there is a world of creatures as wild and dramatic as the cliffs and mountains of the shore. As you wind your way through different habitats, keep an eye out for the "locals." Either a sighting or a sign will let you in on part of the great mystery of this land.

General North Shore History

THE FIRST PEOPLE TO ENTER THE NORTH SHORE region arrived around 10,000 years ago. These Native Americans, called Paleo-Indians, entered the region during the final retreat of the Wisconsin Glaciation. As the Superior ice lobe melted back to the northeast, it blocked the present outlet of Lake Superior, causing lake levels to rise above their present level by up to 450 feet.

This enlarged Lake Superior is known as Glacial Lake Duluth, and in many areas the ancient shoreline closely follows the ridgeline that much of the Superior Hiking Trail now follows. The Paleo-Indians were big game hunters of caribou, bison, musk ox, and possibly mammoth. In all probability, these hunters followed the shoreline of this lake of glacial meltwater along these present-day ridge tops.

The Old Copper Culture followed the Paleo-Indian cultural tradition around Lake Superior and existed from about 5,000 years ago until about 2,000 years ago. During this time the Indians used raw native copper, found on Isle Royale and in northern Michigan, hammering it into tools. Occasionally copper artifacts, in the form of spear points, knives, and fish hooks, are found along the North Shore. If you find copper or stone tools, contact one of the state parks. These finds are very rare and the information will add to the knowledge of this early history.

Many waves of Indian people inhabited the North Shore prior to European contact. The first Europeans, French explorers and fur traders, reached the Lake Superior country about 1620. At that time, the Ojibway (also called Anishinabe or Chippewa) inhabited the eastern end of the lake as far west as the Upper Peninsula of Michigan. Their culture centered at the rapids at the outlet of the big lake. By 1650 the French had encountered the Dakota, or Sioux, at the head of the lake. Along the North Shore lived the Assiniboine and the Cree. As the fur trade moved west over the next 100 years, so did the Ojibway, displacing by 1750 the Dakota, the Assiniboine, and the Cree, who moved farther to the west and north.

By 1780, the Europeans had established fur trading posts at the mouth of the St. Louis River and at Grand Portage. The Ojibway were firmly established on the western end of Lake Superior and in northeastern Minnesota. Both Europeans and Ojibway navigated their frail birch bark canoes along the rugged North Shore between these two important sites of early commerce and, although the Ojibway did have foot trails heading inland at different points along the shore, the early traders had little reason to leave the lake and explore the adjacent uplands.

In 1854, the Ojibway signed the Treaty of La Pointe, which opened up northeastern Minnesota to mineral exploration and settlement. The first permanent settlement was a group of Germans from Ohio who settled at Beaver Bay in 1856. The late 1800s saw a rise of commercial herring fishing along the North Shore and settlement by Scandinavian immigrants. It was said that nearly every cove harbored at least one fisherman's shanty.

Across Lake Superior, Michigan lumber barons had cut most of the big stands of virgin white pine in Michigan by 1890. They then set their sights on Lake Superior's North Shore. Between 1890 and 1910, millions of board feet of red and white pine were cut from the hills along the North Shore. Temporary railroads transported the logs down to Lake Superior where they were rafted up and towed by tugboat to sawmills in Duluth, Superior, Bayfield, and Ashland. Today many of these old railroad grades—most used only for one or two seasons—are still visible. In places, the Superior Hiking Trail either crosses or follows some of these straight and level grades such as the Alger, Nestor and Merrill-Ring grades.

Ever since northeastern Minnesota was opened to exploration, mining has had an active history on the North Shore. Small, unproductive copper explorations began along some of the rivers in the 1850s and 1860s. Beginning in 1884, high-grade iron ore from the Iron Range in northeastern Minnesota was shipped from the huge ore docks in Two Harbors on ore boats bound for the mills on the lower Great Lakes.

At the turn of the century a new company was formed in Two Harbors, Minnesota Mining and Manufacturing. Known today as 3M, the company planned to mine an abrasive rock, misidentified as corundum, at Crystal Bay near the mouth of the Baptism River. At the same time, the North Shore Abrasives Company was formed to mine the same type of rock from a location near Split Rock. In both cases the rock was found to be too soft to serve as an abrasive, and mining operations were discontinued by 1906.

Taconite pellets, refined from low-grade taconite iron ore, were first produced in the mid-1950s from mines on the Mesabi Iron Range. Taconite pellets continue to be processed and shipped to steel plants on the lower Great Lakes from Duluth, Two Harbors, and Silver Bay. Operational railroad tracks crossed by the SHT connect the mines near Ely, Babbitt and Hoyt Lakes with these shipping points along the North Shore.

It is obvious to anyone visiting the North Shore that tourism and recreation have had, and continue to have, a major impact on local development. As early as 1910, when Split Rock Lighthouse was built, the lightkeeper recorded that tourists began visiting the light station by sailboat. Even though a one-lane wagon road was built between certain points along the shore in the 1890s, the present North Shore highway was not completed between Duluth and the Canadian border until 1924. When the highway was completed, camping and cabin resorts sprang up along the shore. Seven state parks were set aside and protected, joined most recently by the eighth, Grand Portage State Park. Today, hikers on the Superior Hiking Trail can still look upon many of the same unspoiled vistas that the Native Americans and the first French explorers saw.

For more information on the cultures and peoples that have inhabited the North Shore, visit the Cook County Historical Society, the Lake County Historical Society, or the Split Rock Lighthouse Visitor Center.

About the Superior Hiking Trail Association

THE SUPERIOR HIKING TRAIL ASSOCIATION (SHTA) is a Minnesota non-profit corporation whose members are dedicated to the completion, preservation, and promotion of the Superior Hiking Trail. The original members of the SHTA were the visionaries—federal and state government representatives and local North Shore resort and business owners—who incorporated the SHTA and obtained the first funding to see their vision become a reality. From this small group, membership has grown to approximately 3,000, including members in 37 states, Canada, and four other foreign countries.

STAFF AND BOARD OF DIRECTORS

The SHTA has a few paid staff members working in the office/store in Two Harbors. Apart from some work performed on contract, the remainder of the work of the SHTA is done by volunteers. A board of directors consisting of members from a variety of locations, careers, avocations, and age groups meets bimonthly on the North Shore to make policy decisions for the SHTA and oversee the substantive work of the association, including trail maintenance, product sales, hikes and event planning, and publications.

ACTIVITIES

The most visible activities of the SHTA are the popular organized hikes scheduled throughout the hiking season, including wintertime snowshoe hikes. Hosted by SHTA members and featuring leaders with interpretive skills, such as naturalists, geologists, photographers, and historians, most of the SHTA-sponsored events are one-way day hikes with an arranged shuttle. The SHTA's hiking program also features backpacking trips of several days. SHTA members also have the opportunity to attend the Annual Meeting, scheduled in May, to participate in a weekend full of hiking, fun, and comraderie.

VOLUNTEERS

Much of the trail was built by crews hired from the local communities and from the Minnesota Conservation Corps (MCC). MCC crews will likely continue to help maintain the SHT. Additional maintenance is provided through a system of volunteers: some have taken responsibility for the upkeep of particular trail sections and campsites; others participate in scheduled maintenance projects. Scout troops, outdoors clubs, and other organizations have all undertaken trail maintenance responsibilities. Individual hikers and groups can give something back to the trail by volunteering to help with trail maintenance. The SHTA will gladly provide you with information on how you can help.

OFFICE AND STORE

The SHTA office and store is located at 731 7th Avenue (the corner of Highway 61 and 8th Street, in a blue-gray Victorian house) in Two Harbors. The store offers a variety of merchandise including guidebooks, maps, t-shirts, sweatshirts, caps, mugs, and other mementos of the SHT. Friendly staff can also answer your questions about the SHT and hike planning. The store is open seven days a week from mid-May to mid-October and Monday through Friday the rest of the year. You can also call or write to receive a store catalog. The address is SHTA, P.O. Box 4, Two Harbors, MN, 55616. The phone number is (218) 834-2700.

WEBSITE

A great deal of information is also available at the SHTA website at www.shta.org. The information includes membership information, store items, trip reports, trail condition updates, and links to lodging, gear, and other useful websites.

MEMBERSHIP

SHTA is a member-based organization of over 3,000 members. We invite you to join SHTA to help build and maintain the Superior Hiking

Trail. Member benefits include free maps of the Trail, *The Ridgeline* newsletter five times a year, and information on guided hikes, maintenance work projects, and the Annual Meeting. The most important benefit is the knowledge you are helping to preserve and protect this wonderful trail. You can join by calling or writing the SHTA office, using the form on the website, or using the form at the back of this book.

A Superior Hiking Trail
Backpacking Primer

BACKPACKING ALLOWS YOU TO EXPERIENCE the Superior Hiking Trail intimately and up close. While this chapter will help hikers enjoy the trail fully and with comfort, experience is the best teacher. Get out there and do it! The goal is to enjoy the hike and the camping. Also, please be sure to read the next chapter on minimum impact trail use and Leave No Trace principles. Using these principles will help protect the SHT well into the future.

There are 81 backcountry campsites located about every five to eight miles along the SHT. Each campsite has 2-8 tent pads, a fire ring, and a backcountry latrine. Some of the campsites are multi-group campsites and are designed for larger groups. There are no reservations, fees, or permits required to use the campsites. Parties are required to share campsites if tent pads are available. Since the trail crosses so much private land and state park land and oftentimes these land ownerships are not marked, campers must camp only at designated campsites.

Please note there is no water source right by a few of the campsites. Also, campsite water sources that are small creeks may be dry by the end of the summer, particularly in a dry year. Water must then be obtained from the nearest river, pond, or lake. Always hang food or use a bearproof container at night or when away from your campsite.

In the trail section descriptions in this guidebook, each campsite is described. Information includes the number of tent pads, the water source for the campsite, and the distance to the previous and next camp-

- Sturdy, comfortable hiking boots
- 2–3 pairs wool socks
- 2 pairs liner socks, silk or synthetic
- Long underwear
- Wool or pile pants
- Lightweight pants, shorts, short and long-sleeved shirts
- Sweater or pile jacket
- Rain jacket or poncho
- Rain pants
- Hat, gloves, gaiters if any probable snow
- Bandana, small towel
- Swim suit (same as shorts, perhaps)
- Sleeping bag
- Stuff sacks
- Foam pad
- Internal or external frame pack
- Sleeping bag lash straps

sites. This information is invaluable in planning your trip. It is a good idea to carry this guidebook or photocopies of the section you are hiking. It can be really useful if the trip doesn't go according to plan (as sometimes happens!) and you need to figure out an alternative.

This guidebook also identifies the trailheads for the beginning and end of each section and describes whether overnight parking is allowed in the parking lot. You can also park a vehicle in the state parks if you have a state park sticker. State park staff will tell you where to park.

GENERAL HIKING TIPS

Regardless of whether you are hiking for a week or an hour, it is always a good idea to let someone know your plans. Tell someone where you plan to hike and when you plan to arrive; then check in when you return. The trail is not patrolled, so your safety or rescue in an emergency may depend on this common-sense precaution.

THROUGH-HIKING THE SUPERIOR HIKING TRAIL

Up to 200 people through-hike the SHT each year. The average time to through-hike the trail is about three weeks, with a mileage of about ten miles a day. The Superior Shuttle can be used to hike from Two Harbors to Judge Magney State Park. After the state park, if hiking unsupported, the trickiest part is getting transportation back from the end of the trail at Otter Lake Road, which is quite remote. Some hikers stop in Grand Marais, find someone to drive them to the end of the trail, and then hike back to Grand Marais. The SHTA office knows of a few people who will provide shuttles for a fee.

There is a bus service provided by H.T. Leasing out of Thunder Bay, Ontario, that stops at most communities along Highway 61 several times a week that can provide transportation for backpacking trips. Their phone number is (807) 473-5955 and their website is www.httours.com/transportation.

To re-supply yourself with food and other items, you can mail packages to Yourself, c/o General Delivery, Town, State, Zip. The package will be held for you for ten days from the date of delivery. Write "Hold for SHTA Hiker" on the package. Below is a chart with communities within two to four miles of the trail and the services they provide.

Another way to re-supply is through the Superior Shuttle. The Shuttle can deliver a package to you at a specified trailhead on a specified date. There are also a couple of outfitters where you can hold packages. The state parks will not hold packages for hikers.

COMMUNITY	ZIP	SERVICES	MEDICAL	MILEPOST
Two Harbors	55616	M, L, G, C, LM, O	Hospital	26.1
Castle Danger	No PO	M, L	—	37.1
Beaver Bay	55601	M, L, LG, LM	—	51.0
Silver Bay	55614	M, L, G, LM, C	Clinic	54.3
Illgen City	No PO	L	—	59.3
Finland	55603	M, L, G, C	—	59.3
Schroeder	55613	L, C	—	79.0
Tofte	55615	M, L, G, O	—	82.6
Lutsen	55612	M, L, G	—	91.7
Grand Marais	55604	M, L, G, C, LM, O	Hospital	109.5

SERVICES
M = meals
L = lodging
G = groceries
LG = limited groceries
C = camping
LM = laundromat
O = outfitting supplies

- Compass
- Map/trail guide/
map case
- Water bottle or
canteen
- Eating utensils:
cup,bowl, plate,
spoon, fork
- Sharp knife
- Flashlight or head-
lamp, extra batteries
- Waterproof matches
or butane lighter
- Candle or firestarter
- Sunglasses
- Sunscreen
- Insect repellent
(mosquitoes, ticks,
black flies)
- First aid kit, with
extra moleskin or
foot care kit
- Toothbrush, comb,
biodegradable
soap, etc.
- 50' nylon cord
- Spare pack parts/
sewing items
- Personal snacks or
lunch food
- Day pack for
side hikes

UNDERSTANDING THE BACKPACKER'S CHECKLIST

The chief nemesis of the sore-hipped, aching-shoulder backpacker is, of course, weight. What to pack, how much to pack, and where in the pack to put it is often-requested information. Use the lists presented here for ideas of what to bring, not as a mandatory agenda. When all is packed, your backpack should weigh no more than one-third of your body weight.

Following are brief explanations of some items noted on the checklist.

Hiking boots. For safe packing and assured ankle support you will need light-weight, over-the-ankle, lug-soled boots, preferably waterproof. Wet boots are usually sloppy fitting and lead to blisters and stumbles. Waterproofness is found in Gore-Tex (or similar material) and full-grain leather boots.

Socks. The most important criterion is fit. Wear what fits well in your boots. A synthetic liner will "wick" moisture away from your foot. A wet foot is a cold foot. Wearing liner socks along with thicker wool socks helps disperse the friction that causes blisters. Let the socks rub against each other, not you.

Long underwear. Synthetic underwear keeps the wearer dry and warm. Leave the long underwear at home if you don't expect cool days or cold nights.

Sweater. Polyester or nylon pile sweaters serve the same function as a wool sweater. They keep you drier, are less bulky, and weigh less than wool.

Rain jacket and pants. Make sure they work. At a minimum they should keep you dry when it's raining. Better yet, they should be something you can wear as an outer shell to break the wind. In this case they should be made of a "waterproof/breathable" fabric.

Other pants, shirts, shorts. You should carry a minimum amount of these. You can change into clean clothes at the car.

Sleeping bags. Better quality down bags are very lightweight, low bulk, retain their loft for many years, and offer the greatest comfort range—from cold nights to hot, humid nights. However, down bags lose their insulating ability when wet. There is a wide range of light-weight synthetic bags now available that retain their loft even when wet.

Stuff sacks. Use the one the sleeping bag comes in filled with clothing as a pillow. Use another inexpensive one for food, another for the cookset. Your sleeping bag should be kept in a truly waterproof stuff sack.

Pack. There is a huge variety of back-packs available, including some designed especially for women. A pack with a good hip belt is essential to help evenly distribute the weight between hips and shoulders. It's very important to try on the pack before you purchase it and to adjust the pack to your torso. There is also a new selection of ultra-light packs available, which can really help to bring the weight of the pack down. Be sure that even a light pack has a good hip belt or you may find you have really sore shoulders once you've carried the pack for several days.

BACKPACKER'S CAMPING EQUIPMENT LIST: Group Equipment

- Tent with rain fly
- Ground tarp for tent
- Tent stakes
- Lightweight cooking stove
- Fuel and fuel containers (1 pint per week per person)
- Fuel funnel (if necessary)
- Cook set
- Scrub pad, biodegradable soap
- Pot grippers
- Community food (lots of it)
- Cooking grate for fires (check current regulations on campfires)
- Water purification tablets or water filter

Tent. Lightweight, sturdy, dry…is that too much to ask? Look for freestanding designs. They are easy to pitch and shed wind well. Dryness is related to fabric quality, sealed seams and ventilation. A good tent will not only keep rain out, but also let your body heat and vapor out from inside. Look for design features that allow for venting, even during a downpour. A tarp sized a bit smaller than your tent floor can be put under the tent to protect the floor.

Stoves. Lightweight one-burner stoves are mandatory. The easiest to use are those with fuel in sealed canisters, such as butane, iso-butane or other fuels. The canister plugs into the burner and with a twist of the knob and one match you've got a flame. Unfortunately these stoves often don't put out enough heat and they can work poorly in subfreezing weather. Gasoline burning stoves are more versatile; you carry the fuel in a refillable fuel bottle. This is more ecologically sound and your stove will work in all weather conditions. The disadvantage of these stoves is that they are sometimes fickle and may require preheating with fire paste or liquid fuel. Look for ones that both simmer well and bring water to a quick boil.

Food. Be prepared to carry lots of extra weight if you want to have fun making meals from scratch. The lightweight alternatives, freeze-dried foods, are very easy to prepare but also relatively expensive. You don't need to purchase freeze-dried foods, however. You can find a large variety of lightweight meals in the rice/pasta convenience food section of any grocery store.

For lunches, bagels can withstand heaps of abuse. Nuts, cheeses, salami, jams, peanut butter, and cream cheese are all good bets. Also try the huge selection of energy bars.

Breakfasts can be as simple as oatmeal or granola with powdered milk. Pancakes are excellent if you don't need to get moving quickly.

Water. All drinking water must be boiled, filtered or chemically treated. Iodine tablets are the best chemical treatment but the water will taste of iodine. Backcountry filters are considered to be the best option because they remove all harmful bacteria, giardia, and funny tastes. Look for filters that are self-cleaning and easy to use.

Fun accessories. Some things aren't essential but are fun to take along anyway. Bring one or two. Examples: boomerangs, Frisbees, Hacky Sacks, cards, games, harmonicas, chairs, books, solar showers, cameras, film, altimeters, etc.

Packing the pack. Get everything as close to your center of gravity as possible. Pack your sleeping bag at the bottom, next heavier things, and then lighter things above your shoulders

No pack is truly waterproof. You should use waterproof stuff sacks for your gear and/or use pack liners (garbage bags work) or pack covers if you want bone-dry performance.

Procedures for food and garbage. Never take any food into your tent at night. Hoist all of your food and garbage in its stuff sack into a tree. It should end up hanging 10 feet off the ground and 5 feet from the tree trunk. Use a rock tied to the end of your rope to get the rope slung over a high sturdy branch, then tie the food bag to one end of the rope. Pull the other end until the bag is suspended, then tie off that end to the tree trunk. When leaving camp be sure to pack out all food debris. Any garbage left in the campsite is a potential attraction for bears. Once a bear finds food at a campsite, he is likely to return and could cause a problem for other campers using the site.

Think about weight. Backpacking can be as much work or as little work as you make it. If you can carry a minimum of frills, your pack can weigh less than 30 pounds for a one-week trip and you will enjoy walking ten miles or more per day. Or…you can bring all kinds of heavy gear, which allows for deluxe camping but may lead to sore shoulders after only six miles of walking. You need to decide what works best for you.

Minimum Impact Trail Use: Leave No Trace

AS MORE AND MORE HIKERS AND BACKPACKERS use the Superior Hiking Trail, minimizing impacts is crucial to protecting the trail and the natural environment of the trail. The Superior Hiking Trail Association supports a set of principles called the Leave No Trace principles and encourages all trail users to follow them. These guidelines are in place to help protect the environment and a high quality hiking experience. Below are guidelines adapted for the Superior Hiking Trail:

PLAN AHEAD AND PREPARE

Know the type of terrain and the range of weather conditions you might encounter. Be prepared for any emergencies you might encounter. Always use a map when hiking on the trail. Know and respect the rules for the trail.

TRAVEL AND CAMP ON DURABLE SURFACES

Use the existing main trail and spur trails. Stay on the trail at all times on signed private lands and in signed sensitive areas. Always walk single file and avoid shortcuts to avoid damage to the trail and surrounding area. Walk through mud puddles to avoid widening the trail. Never blaze trees or use other markers.

Use the designated campsites and plan your trip mileage to use designated campsites. Camping at the campsites is on a first-come, first-use basis. Parties are asked to share campsites if tent pads are available. Camping is absolutely prohibited on private lands and in state parks. Use the tent pads that have been cleared and do not make new ones. Do not trench around the tent.

DISPOSE OF WASTE PROPERLY

Pack it in, pack it out. Pack out all trash, leftover food, and litter. Inspect your campsite and rest areas for trash or spilled foods. Seal all waste in airtight containers and hang it with your food bag each night. Pick up trash others have left. Never bury garbage.

Use the latrines located at each campsite and dispose of toilet paper only in the latrines. Pack out all sanitary products. If you aren't near a latrine, dig a small hole for human waste 3-6 inches deep at least 200 feet from a water source. Fill it in and camouflage when finished.

Never use soap in a lake or stream—carry water 200 feet from water sources to wash dishes or yourself. Dispose of dishwater well away from a water source and from your campsite.

LEAVE WHAT YOU FIND

Leave rocks, plants and other natural objects as you find them. Do not touch or take cultural or historic structures or artifacts.

MINIMIZE CAMPFIRE IMPACTS

Use a lightweight stove for cooking and enjoy a small candle lantern for light. If you make a fire, make it only in the fire ring provided at each campsite. If you are sharing the campsite with another party, do not build a second fire. Burn only small diameter wood found on the ground. Do not damage live trees. Never take birch bark from trees. Be sure your campfire is completely out before you leave camp.

RESPECT WILDLIFE

Observe wildlife from a distance. Do not try to attract or approach wild animals. Never feed animals human food. This disrupts their natural food cycle. Pets must be on leash at all times to avoid disturbing wildlife. Always hang your food and garbage (or keep in a bear-proof container) at night or when away from your campsite to avoid attracting wildlife.

BE CONSIDERATE OF OTHER VISITORS

Respect other visitors and protect the quality of their experience. Yield to other users on the trail. Let nature's sounds prevail. Avoid loud voices and noises. Be courteous when sharing a campsite with another party.

The Best of the
Superior Hiking Trail

EVERY SECTION OF THE SUPERIOR HIKING TRAIL is the best...for some reason. Over the years, some sections have become better known than others. People have voted with their feet for favorites like Oberg Mountain in the fall. Here are suggestions for your hiking selection.

CROWD FAVORITES

These sections are scenic and easy to reach. They are popular for good reason. Be prepared for great hiking and a few other folks along the trail. Some of these hikes are loops and some of them are out-and-back hikes.

- Split Rock River Loop: Up and down the banks of this spirited river (5.0 miles, see page 62-65).

- Bean and Bear Lakes Loop (also called the Twin Lakes Trail): Climb to a mountainous setting and enjoy the scenic lakes below (6.6 or 7.6 mile loops, see pages 76-80).

- Mount Trudee: A challenging uphill climb to spectacular views in Tettegouche State Park (4.8 miles one-way from Tettegouche, see pages 81-83).

- Carlton Peak: A steep climb to one of the highest mountains in Minnesota (3.1 miles one-way from Temperance River, 1.7 miles one-way from Sawbill Trail, see pages 116-119).

- Oberg Mountain Loop: A great meander to scenic views, especially in fall colors (1.8 mile loop, see page 126).

LOOPS

No need to shuttle or return along the same trail with these routes.

- Caribou River: From trailhead go up one side of the river, cross the bridge beyond the falls, and return on the other side (1.5 miles, see page 105-107).
- Cascade River: Go up one side of the river to Co. Rd. 45 and return on the other (7.8 miles, see page 140-145).
- Cove Point Loop: The spur trail goes from Cove Point Lodge up to the radio tower, then makes a scenic loop along Fault Line Ridge and returns to the Lodge (5.8 miles, see page 71).

BIKE SHUTTLES

If you have just one car but want to hike through a section, bring a bike for the shuttle. Park your bike at the end of the section and drive to the start. Do your hike and then bike back to your vehicle.

- From Gooseberry Falls State Park to Castle Danger.
- From Beaver Bay to Silver Bay. Ride along Penn Blvd. (Co. Rd. 5) and Co. Rd. 4.
- From Temperance River State Park to Cook Co. Rd. 1.
- From Arrowhead Trail to Jackson Lake Rd.

WILDERNESS TREKS

Long-distance sections with fewer people along the trail.
- Split Rock to Beaver Bay.
- Finland Recreation Center to Crosby-Manitou State Park.
- Crosby-Manitou State Park to Caribou River.
- Cascade River State Park to Bally Creek Rd.
- Jackson Lake Rd. to Otter Lake Rd.

SCENIC SHORTIES

Shorter walks to scenic spots.
- Wolf Rock from Castle Danger trailhead (0.5 miles one-way, see pages 51-54).
- Highway 1 to Fantasia overlooks (1.2 miles one-way, see pages 84-86).

- Lake Co. Rd. 6 to Section 13 cliffs (1.3 miles one-way, see pages 88-90).
- Cook Co. Rd. 58 to Devil Track River (1 mile one-way, see pages 154-155).
- Kadunce River (0.7 miles one-way, see pages 162-163).
- Lakewalk section (1.6 miles one-way, see page 165).

BEST TROUT FISHING

Cross the river on a scenic bridge and toss a lure.
- Gooseberry River
- Split Rock River
- Manitou River
- Cascade River
- Poplar River

MOST DRAMATIC PEAKS
- Mount Trudee
- Carlton Peak
- Oberg Mountain
- Ridgeline between Arrowhead Trail and Jackson Lake Rd.

Map Legend

Superior Hiking Trail

Spur trails or other trails

Parking areas **P**

Backcountry campsites, SHT ▲

Multi-group campsites, SHT Ⓜ

Major campgrounds, State Park/commercial Ⓒ

Text descriptions correspond to
reference points on maps ◄

Main road ▬▬▬▬▬▬

Other road ....

State Park boundary — · — · — · — · —

State highway 61

Major county highway ⑦

Forest service, township roads
or other county roads 158 ◇617◇

NORTH is always to the top of the page. The SHT runs
primarily in a SW to NE direction.

SCALE 1" = 1 MILE
The gridwork visible on the gray base map indicates
one-mile square sections.

Lake County Road 301
to Castle Danger

START (END)
Lake Co. Rd. 301 (Fors Rd.)

END (START)
Silver Creek Township Rd. 617
(West Castle Danger Rd.)

LENGTH OF TRAIL SECTION
6.3 miles

SAFETY CONCERNS
• Some steep walking in Crow
  Creek ravine

ACCESS AND PARKING
Nearest Hwy. 61 milepost: 28.5

Secondary road name and number: Lake Co. Rd. 3

Follow Lake Co. Rd. 3 for
2.0 miles. Turn left on Lake Co.
Rd. 301 (Fors Rd.) for 0.3 miles
to trailhead parking lot.
Overnight okay.

FACILITIES
At starting trailhead (farthest
southwest): none

Designated campsites on this
section of SHT: none

SYNOPSIS
The trail runs from rolling
valleys up to rocky, pine-studded
ridgelines. The Encampment
River is a scenic halfway point,
while the stunted trees and
expansive views to the east are
reminiscent of a hike at timberline in the Rockies. A 1.2-mile
spur trail from the trailhead
offers a nice hike to scenic
Silver Creek.

MILE-BY-MILE DESCRIPTION

0.0 (6.3)
LAKE CO. RD. 301 (FORS RD.)

SHT heads easterly in fir-dominated woods, soon descending past big spruces to a branch of Silver Creek. It continues east along an old ditch in open woods and an overgrown field, soon coming to Lake Co. Rd. 3, lined with planted pines.

SPUR TRAIL WEST FROM TRAILHEAD:

There is a 1.2-mile spur trail that travels west from the Co. Rd. 301 trailhead parking lot to scenic Silver Creek with a campsite on the creek. This is a nice option if you reach the trailhead late in the day or if you simply want a scenic stroll.

▲ SILVER CREEK CAMPSITE

TYPE: Regular
TENT PADS: 3
WATER: From Silver Creek
SETTING: Northeast side of Silver Creek,
    1.2 miles west of Co. Rd. 301
NEXT CAMPSITE: 8.8 miles

0.7 (5.6)
LAKE CO. RD. 3

SHT crosses the highway at an angle and soon crosses an ATV trail, then descends steeply to the bridge over Wilson Creek. A few big old yellow birches and a small grove of cedars enhance the creek bottom. SHT then climbs back out to the flat upland at the edge of an old field dotted with spruce and fir. It temporarily joins an ATV trail at a dip, rising slightly in mixed woods with some ash and balsam poplar in the wetter spots. A few young sugar maples add diversity as SHT approaches Silver Creek Township Rd. 613.

1.1 (5.2)
SILVER CREEK 613 (LOOP RD.)

SHT departs from 613 through a mixed forest of ash, aspen, and alder, then climbs gradually, crossing road to radio communication tower, over a rocky ridge and down through thick balsam, crossing the old Beaver Bay Rd. and a small creek before a steep climb.

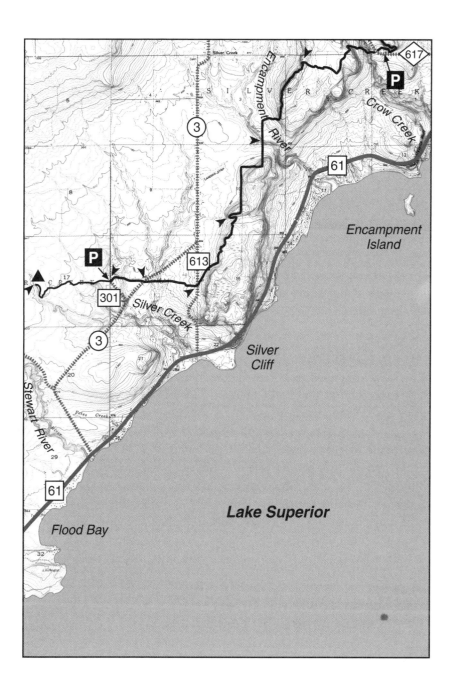

2.3 (4.0)
PINE RIDGE OVERLOOK

Views of the Two Harbors area to the west from a ridge of red pines and spruce. SHT then passes through private land, running due north-south and then due east-west through white pine and cedar. Hikers are asked to be respectful of owner's rights and stay on the SHT. No camping or fires on private land.

3.6 (2.7)
ENCAMPMENT RIVER CROSSING

SHT descends to the bridge crossing, then climbs to top of ridge east of the Encampment River, then continues along a ridgeline, with views of the Silver Creek, Stewart, and Encampment River valleys. The dwarfed spruces and pines and the mossy ground combine with the wide view to give this section the feel of hiking at timberline in high mountains.

4.3 (2.0)
RED PINE OVERLOOK

Wide view from a red-pine framed outcrop into valley below before SHT turns into the forest and down into a low, wet area. SHT continues into a mixed maple forest. A scenic view (with a bench) across the Crow Creek valley includes pine-studded Wolf Rock. This is private land, so please respect the owner's rights. Wooden steps lead steeply into the river gorge. Note the visible flows of rock in the cliffs of the creek. A 40-foot footbridge crosses Crow Creek, then SHT climbs a talus slope. Watch for "Poison Ivy" sign along the slope. This is the only place along SHT where poison ivy may be found. SHT continues through birches, crosses Silver Creek Township Rd. 617, then skirts base of Wolf Rock's dramatic cliffs into parking lot.

6.3 (0.0)
SILVER CREEK TOWNSHIP RD. 617
(WEST CASTLE DANGER RD.) PARKING LOT

Castle Danger to Gooseberry Falls State Park

START (END)
Silver Creek Township Rd. 617 (West Castle Danger Rd.), north of Castle Danger

END (START)
Gooseberry Falls State Park Visitor Center

LENGTH OF TRAIL SECTION
9.1 miles

SAFETY CONCERNS
• Rocky cliffs at Wolf Rock—keep children in hand

• Possible trail erosion along meandering Gooseberry River

ACCESS AND PARKING
Nearest Hwy. 61 milepost: 36.6. Intersection marked by SHTA sign.

Secondary road name and number: Lake Co. Rd. 106 (West Castle Danger Rd.), which becomes Silver Creek Township Rd. 617 after 0.6 miles.

Go 2.4 miles on Lake Co. Rd. 106/Silver Creek Township Rd. 617. Lot is on right. Overnight okay.

FACILITIES
At starting trailhead (farthest southwest): none

Designated campsites on this section of SHT: four

SYNOPSIS
This section starts with a short but steep climb to the ridgeline and Wolf Rock. It is the quickest way on any section of the trail to get to outstanding ridgeline views. After descending from the ridgeline and going through mixed forest, the trail ascends once more to Mike's Rock with more scenic vistas. The true highlight of the section is four miles of trail along the Gooseberry River, with its meandering course and a series of dramatic waterfalls.

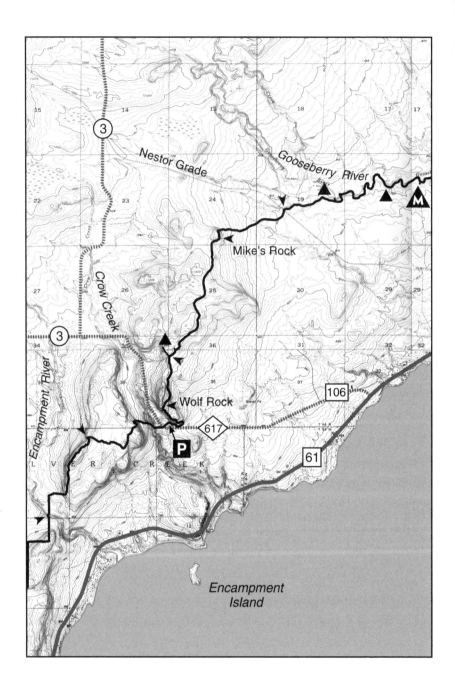

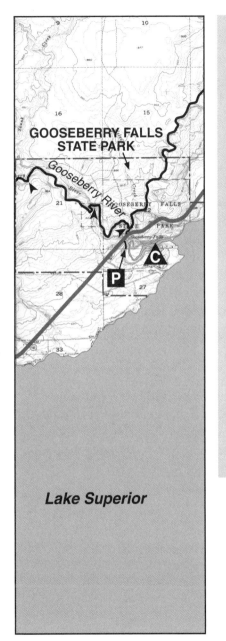

GOOSEBERRY FALLS STATE PARK

Gooseberry River

Lake Superior

BERRIES OF THE
SUPERIOR HIKING TRAIL

Many hikers indulge in the satisfying experience of eating as they hike along the Superior Hiking Trail. Several species of berries are common along the trail, and they ripen from July to September. Blueberries are frequent on the rocky outcrops and scenic overlooks. These, as well as other sweet fruit species, need the full sun that is available on the hill crests. But don't limit your foraging to blueberries; keep your eyes peeled for strawberries, raspberries, thimbleberries, and juneberries. Bring along a bag or bucket—and remember, some berries are poisonous so eat only fruit that you know.

MILE-BY-MILE DESCRIPTION

0.0 (9.1)
SILVER CREEK 617 PARKING LOT

SHT departs right side of parking lot, winds up through cliffs to the top of Wolf Rock. This is one of the most dramatic first half-miles of the SHT as the trail winds up to top of Wolf Rock with its pine-clad rock outcrops.

0.5 (8.6)
WOLF ROCK

Great views at 1,200 feet of Lake Superior, Crow Creek valley, forests, etc. On ridge, SHT passes through a mile of private land. Hikers are asked to be respectful and stay on the SHT. No camping or fires on private land. SHT turns away from the valley as the woods alternate from open understory to dense growth. Lots of dead birch in this section, plus large mammal signs. Decomposed lava looks like gravel on the trailbed. Trail is wide with some mud holes when wet.

1.1 (8.0)
SPUR TRAIL TO OVERLOOK

215 yards to vista overlooking Crow Creek valley. SHT continues along ridge, departing private land, through a cedar grove that is the source of a stream, and up and down some rocky spots. The woods alternate from open understory to a dense growth enclosing the trail in a "green tunnel."

▲ CROW CREEK VALLEY CAMPSITE

TYPE: Regular
TENT PADS: 5
WATER: From small stream, unreliable in dry periods
SETTING: 1.3 miles north of Silver Creek 617
NEXT CAMPSITE: 3.4 miles

2.9 (6.2)
MIKE'S ROCK

Vistas north and east to Gooseberry River Valley and Lake Superior. SHT descends with stone steps past outcrops to low area of open birch and maple, crosses small stream and marshy area. Some dead birch in here, due to cumulative stress of drought, damage by birch leaf miner beetle and tent caterpillars.

4.0 (5.1)
NESTOR GRADE CROSSING

This is an old logging railroad that was used for transporting logs to Lake Superior, and used now by ATVs. SHT climbs to higher, drier ground and a beautiful stand of birch trees. Berry bushes abundant, including raspberry and thimbleberry. SHT crosses several intermittent streams and reaches overlook of the Gooseberry River. Lots of beaver signs.

4.7 (4.4)
GOOSEBERRY RIVER AND CAMPSITE

Note gravel bars along river—this is a good source of agates. SHT continues along river, with interesting meanders and oxbow cutoffs. The trail is subject to flooding in the floodplain. These two miles of the SHT are particularly beautiful in the fall and early spring. Many paths where beaver drag branches to water. Also, watch for migrating waterfowl in spring and fall.

▲ WEST GOOSEBERRY CAMPSITE

TYPE: Regular
TENT PADS: 4
WATER: From Gooseberry River
SETTING: 3.9 miles from Gooseberry Falls, on a hill
PREVIOUS CAMPSITE: 3.4 miles
NEXT CAMPSITE: 0.9 miles

▲ EAST GOOSEBERRY CAMPSITE

TYPE: Regular
TENT PADS: 2
WATER: From Gooseberry River
SETTING: 3.0 miles from Gooseberry Falls, on a small knoll
PREVIOUS CAMPSITE: 0.9 miles
NEXT CAMPSITE: 0.8 miles

GOOSEBERRY FALLS STATE PARK

Rocky Lake Superior shoreline and five waterfalls highlight Gooseberry Falls State Park. The park was established in 1933, and the Civilian Conservation Corps developed the park between 1934 and 1941, including the stone buildings, campground, picnic area, and trails. These structures have earned Gooseberry Falls State Park a place on the National Register of Historic Places. Today the park covers 1,675 acres and includes a 70-site drive-in campground, a rustic group camp at the former CCC camp location, and 18 miles of hiking trails (including a self-guided trail along the Gooseberry River). The visitor center and wayside rest off of Highway 61 serves as an interpretive center and nature store. Its selection of quality outdoor education material is unsurpassed in the area. Interpretive programs are provided during the summer and include guided walks, activities, and evening programs.

GOOSEBERRY RIVER MULTI-GROUP CAMPSITE

TYPE: Multi-group
TENT PADS: 8
WATER: From Gooseberry River
SETTING: 2.2 miles from Gooseberry Falls trailhead, 30 yards off of river
PREVIOUS CAMPSITE: 0.8 miles
NEXT CAMPSITE: 5.3 miles (or use Gooseberry Falls State Park Campground)

6.8 (2.3) JUNCTION WITH PARK TRAIL

Wide, grassy trail follows river for a distance, past shelter and up the hill. Trail junction has arrows and "You are here" sign. Pass ten foot fence which protects young trees from deer damage, called a "deer exclosure." Trail turns sharp left to river and crosses bridge at Fifth Falls.

8.0 (1.1) FIFTH FALLS BRIDGE

After crossing river SHT follows park's Fifth Falls Trail along east side of Gooseberry River.

8.9 (0.2) JUNCTION WITH SPUR TRAIL

Main SHT turns sharply to the left just before the old Visitors

Center (stone building) and heads northeast to Split Rock River on wide ski trail.

To go from here to Visitor Center and parking lot, turn right, go past the old Visitor Center, continue on paved trail, and take the pedestrian bridge over the Gooseberry River. Continue on to Visitor Center and parking lot.

9.1 (0.0)
GOOSEBERRY FALLS STATE PARK VISITOR CENTER

Gooseberry Falls State Park to Split Rock River Wayside

START (END)
Gooseberry Falls State Park Visitors Center

END (START)
Split Rock River Wayside on Hwy. 61

LENGTH OF TRAIL SECTION
6.0 miles

SAFETY CONCERNS
None

ACCESS AND PARKING
Nearest Hwy. 61 milepost: 38.9

Secondary road name and number: none

Park at Gooseberry Falls State Park Visitor Center. Plenty of parking available. No overnight parking at wayside area. Overnight parking available in state park with park sticker. Check in at Contact Station going to campground.

FACILITIES
At starting trailhead (farthest southwest): bathrooms, snacks, telephone, drinking water

Designated campsites on this section of trail: one

SYNOPSIS
This section starts out traveling through a variety of forests. It then climbs to and follows Bread Loaf Ridge with stunning views of Lake Superior making this section one of the best views on the SHT. The easy descent into the Split Rock River Valley is also quite spectacular.

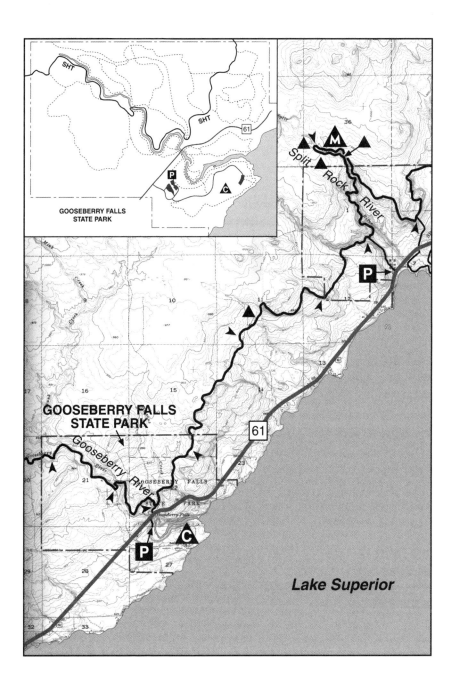

GOOSEBERRY FALLS STATE PARK

SHT

SHT

61

P

C

GOOSEBERRY FALLS
STATE PARK

Split

Rock

River

M

P

61

GOOSEBERRY FALLS
STATE PARK

Gooseberry River

GOOSEBERRY FALLS
STATE PARK

P

C

Lake Superior

MILE-BY-MILE DESCRIPTION

0.0 (6.0)
GOOSEBERRY FALLS STATE PARK VISITOR CENTER

Spur trail follows state park trail on pedestrian bridge across the Gooseberry River and past the old visitors center, where it intersects main SHT. On ski trails, it travels through birch and pine, up a high rise and across Nelson's Creek. The trail is well marked at junctions with other ski trails. SHT leaves ski trail and continues on hiking trail to state park boundary.

1.2 (4.8)
SHT SIGN

SHT goes through aspen, birch, and cedar, and then follows a gentle downhill leveling out in a cedar grove. Sign notes contribution of Philip Economon family. SHT follows base of ridge through lovely birch forest and crosses five small footbridges across creeks. SHT travels through nice stand of white pines.

PUBLIC-PRIVATE COOPERATION

We take things for granted sometimes—like a clearly marked trail, or a footbridge over a low wet area. In fact, some things we almost can't help but take for granted because we never learn about them. For example, private landowners have helped make the Superior Hiking Trail a reality by sharing their property. More than 10% of the trail crosses land that is privately owned. Less than 1% crosses property of the Superior Hiking Trail Association. As you hike the trail, please remember that you are often a guest!

2.8 (3.2)
BLUEBERRY HILL RD.

SHT crosses dirt road, goes through birch and poplar, crosses split log footbridge, passes a campsite, then climbs small hill to cedar grove.

▲ BLUEBERRY HILL CAMPSITE

TYPE: Regular
TENT PADS: 4
WATER: From creek, right at campsite,
    unreliable in dry periods
SETTING: 0.1 miles east of Blueberry Hill Rd.
PREVIOUS CAMPSITE: 5.3 miles (or use Gooseberry Falls State Park)
NEXT CAMPSITE: 4.0 miles

3.4 (2.6)
BREAD LOAF OVERLOOK

After a short but steep climb marked by two arrow signs, the trail comes out onto a ridge with a stunning overlook of Lake Superior and forest. The ridge, with weathered rock, reindeer lichen, and wild roses, continues for almost a mile. Rock cairns mark the trail in rocky areas. The trail descends into the Split Rock River valley. It continues up a steep grade into Split Rock Lighthouse State Park (note sign) and then follows an easy descent through beautiful birch groves. The trail passes by the top of a waterfall on West Branch of Split Rock River.

5.5 (0.5)
WATERFALL AND TRAIL JUNCTION

At junction, go left to continue on main SHT or right on spur trail 0.5 miles to Hwy. 61.

6.0 (0.0)
SPLIT ROCK RIVER WAYSIDE ON HWY. 61

SHTA kiosk and map in parking lot.

Split Rock River Loop

START (END)
Split Rock River Wayside

END (START)
Split Rock River Wayside

LENGTH OF TRAIL SECTION
5.0 miles

SAFETY CONCERNS
• One steep rock ascent/descent on west side of river.

ACCESS AND PARKING
Nearest Hwy. 61 milepost: 43.5

Secondary road name and number: none

Wayside rest on west side of Split Rock River. No overnight parking allowed at wayside rest.

FACILITIES
At starting trailhead (farthest southwest): none

Designated campsites on this section of SHT: four

SYNOPSIS
This is one of the premier day-hike loops on the SHT. The attractive trail ascends the west side of the river, which cascades down to Lake Superior. The river cascades past cliffs and through clefts of sheer red rock walls draped with conifers. After crossing the bridge, the trail affords some beautiful views of the river valley. The SHT then leaves the river and goes through forest until reaching a park shelter with a commanding overlook of Lake Superior and the river valley.

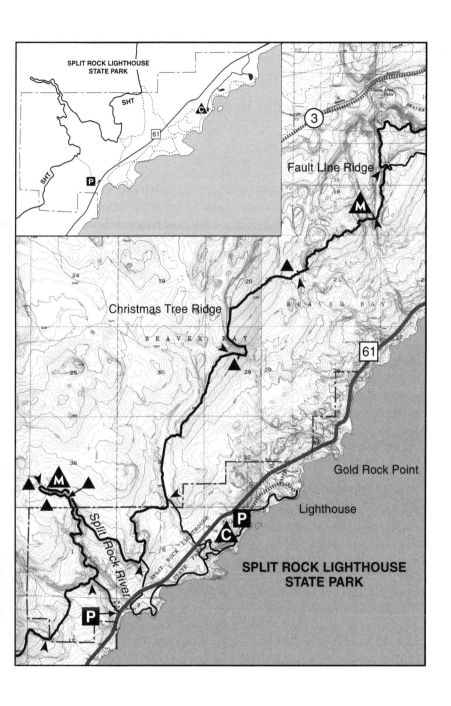

Split Rock River

Christmas Tree Ridge

Fault Line Ridge

Beaver Bay

Gold Rock Point

Lighthouse

SPLIT ROCK LIGHTHOUSE STATE PARK

SPLIT ROCK LIGHTHOUSE STATE PARK

SHT

61

3

MILE-BY-MILE DESCRIPTION

0.0 (5.0)
TRAILHEAD ON WEST SIDE OF SPLIT ROCK RIVER

Spur to SHT climbs gradually, with views of river valley to the east.

0.5 (4.5)
JUNCTION WITH SHT

Watch for sharp right turn from spur trail to main trail. Gorgeous waterfall just past junction of Southwest Branch of Split Rock River, also a semi-cave carved by the creek. SHT becomes more difficult after junction, climbing short, steep hills. Watch for washouts and steep overlooks. SHT winds through some impressive rock formations, including a chimney formation known as the Pillars. Many waterfalls are passed along the way. Watch for a large rock outcrop in the middle of the river which splits the flow of the river around a tree-studded island.

▲ SOUTHWEST SPLIT ROCK RIVER CAMPSITE

TYPE: Regular
TENT PADS: 4
WATER: From Split Rock River
SETTING: 0.5 miles from footbridge, on west side of river
PREVIOUS CAMPSITE: 4.0 miles
NEXT CAMPSITE: 0.4 miles

▲ NORTHWEST SPLIT ROCK RIVER CAMPSITE

TYPE: Regular
TENT PADS: 3
WATER: From Split Rock River
SETTING: Right before footbridge on west side of river,
   in a grove of cedar trees on a small hill
PREVIOUS CAMPSITE: 0.4 miles
NEXT CAMPSITE: 0.2 miles

2.6(2.4)
SPLIT ROCK RIVER CROSSING

East side of Split Rock River is more open, with conifers and bare rock. The river cascades through attractive red rock canyon walls topped with conifers. Partial views of Lake Superior as the trail enters mixed birch/aspen forest. The trail reaches wide overlook, with view of Lake Superior, highway, and lighthouse. Adirondack shelter marks junction with state park ski trails.

⚠ NORTHEAST SPLIT ROCK RIVER CAMPSITE

TYPE: Multi-group
TENT PADS: 7
WATER: From Split Rock River
SETTING: 0.3 miles south of foot-
    bridge on east side of river,
    in a grove of large aspen trees
PREVIOUS CAMPSITE: 0.2 miles
NEXT CAMPSITE: 0.3 miles

▲ SOUTHEAST SPLIT ROCK RIVER CAMPSITE

TYPE: Regular
TENT PADS: 2
WATER: From Split Rock River
SETTING: 0.6 miles south of foot-
    bridge on east side of river,
    across from the stone pillars
PREVIOUS CAMPSITE: 0.3 miles
NEXT CAMPSITE: 4.7 miles

4.3 (0.7)
JUNCTION WITH SPUR BACK TO HWY. 61

Follow spur trail back down to Hwy. 61 and finish loop. Spur trail is a XC trail but is maintained for hiking. This would be quite a ski run! Turn right at highway and walk along shoulder inside guard rail to return to parking lot.

5.0 (0.0) HWY. 61 PARKING LOT

GEOLOGY OF SPLIT ROCK RIVER

The reddish-tan color of the rock in the Split Rock River gorge is quite a contrast to the more typi-cal dark gray to black colors of the basalts of the North Shore.
This rock, known as rhyolite, formed from a massive lava flow. As the flow cooled, it developed vertical cracks, or "columnar joints," similar to those at Palisade Head, as well as many smaller horizontal cracks. Postglacial river erosion of the last 11,000 years, made easy by all these fractures, has eaten deeply into the flow, but has left some columns isolated right alongside the trail. Frost action over the centuries produces the "shingle" effect of loose chips and slabs on the rock surface and along the trail.

Split Rock River Wayside to Beaver Bay

START (END)
Split Rock River Wayside at Split Rock River or State Park Trail Center

END (START)
Lake Co. Rd. 4 (Lax Lake Rd.) north of Beaver Bay

LENGTH OF TRAIL SECTION
11.3 miles from east side of river

SAFETY CONCERNS
• Steep climbs near Fault Line Ridge

ACCESS AND PARKING
There are two starting trailheads:

1) Split Rock River Wayside, milepost 43.5. Walk from parking lot 200 yards northeast along highway (behind guard rail) to start of spur trail.

2) Follow spur trail from Trail Center inside Split Rock Lighthouse State Park. Milepost 45.9. Overnight parking at Trail Center okay (permit required).

FACILITIES
At starting trailhead (farthest southwest): none

Services available at Split Rock Lighthouse State Park: bathrooms, water, phone, etc.

Designated campsites on this section of the SHT: three

SYNOPSIS
A challenging rocky trail affording dramatic views both of Lake Superior and inland. In many places the SHT follows along the edge of high escarpments with conifers clinging precariously 300 to 400 feet above the valley floor. There are many steep ascents and descents that take one through a wide variety of forests—much birch, maple, and aspen as well as impressive stands of cedars and white pines. The section also traverses part of the Merrill Grade, one of the historic logging railroads. Many sections of the SHT traverse long ridges of table rock, or follow long outcroppings which form walls for the SHT. In one area hikers must proceed carefully along a pond bounded with large rocks and small boulders. There is also a 5.8-mile loop from Cove Point Lodge in the middle of this section.

MILE-BY-MILE DESCRIPTION

0.0 (11.3)
TRAILHEAD ON EAST SIDE OF SPLIT ROCK RIVER, ON HWY. 61
Spur trail climbs up wide state park XC trails to junction marked with sign.

0.5 (10.8)
JUNCTION WITH SHT
Turn right to head towards Beaver Bay. SHT follows ridgeline, passing two good vistas of Lake Superior and lighthouse, then descends. Some of the rock outcrops are old shorelines of Glacial Lake Duluth. The long gentle descent leads to a low, boggy area, then the junction with a ski trail, then a wide ski trail bridge over Split Rock Creek.

1.7 (9.6)
JUNCTION WITH SPUR TO STATE PARK CAMPGROUND
Soon after crossing creek, 1.4-mile spur from state park campground joins SHT. SHT soon joins old Merrill Grade railroad route. SHT follows moss-covered remains of old railroad ties through birch, aspen, and balsam. Watch for sign where SHT departs grade. SHT climbs to long walk along exposed rock ridge with spruce and lichen-covered rocks and steep drops to north. SHT crosses ATV trail at 3.0 miles. Large pines between the trail and view of Lake Superior.

3.4 (7.9)
CHAPINS RIDGE CAMPSITE
Just east of campsite SHT follows 30-foot wooden stairway and crosses stream on split log bridge. SHT crosses logging road, then climbs to overlook atop Christmas Tree Ridge through open grassy area. Good views inland. SHT continues in open area, through a fine stand of white pines, and descends from ridge through brush and aspen, and past a pond.

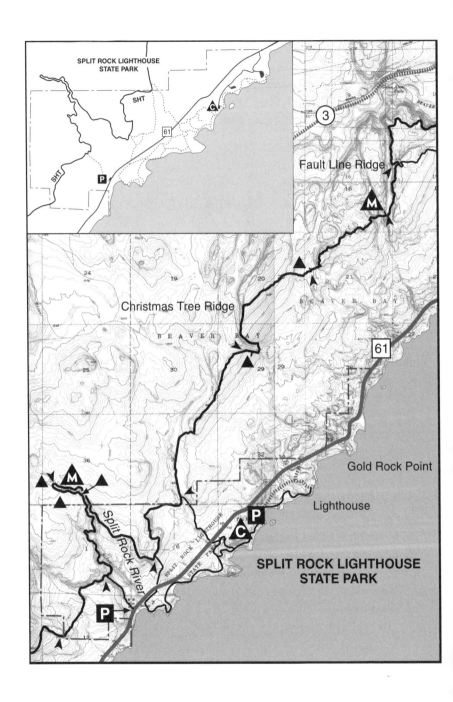

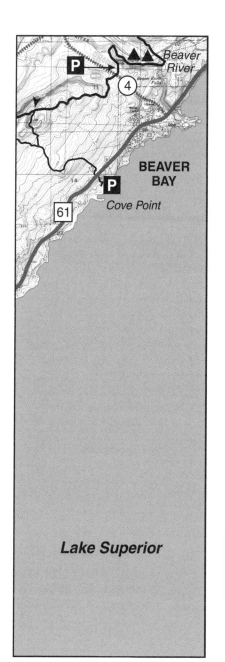

SPLIT ROCK LIGHTHOUSE STATE PARK

Established as a park in 1971, today Split Rock Lighthouse State Park includes 2,075 acres along Lake Superior between the Split Rock River and the lighthouse. The park hosts a number of historic sites including a commercial fishing village site, an early mine site, the site of a logging camp and dam, and of course the lighthouse and surrounding buildings. One of the unique aspects of the park is the cart-in campground. Campers cart in rather than drive in to the 20 sites located along Lake Superior. Four lakeside backpack sites are also available. Twelve miles of trails connect and follow the lakeshore and the ridge 600 feet above. Another popular pastime, fishing, especially for trout and salmon, is excellent along the Split Rock River.

▲ CHAPINS RIDGE CAMPSITE

TYPE: Regular
TENT PADS: 4
WATER: 0.2 miles away at
    Chapins Creek
SETTING: 1.5 miles east of Merrill
    Grade
PREVIOUS CAMPSITE: 4.7 miles
NEXT CAMPSITE: 2.2 miles

5.6 (5.7)
BEAVER POND CAMPSITE

SHT passes large beaver pond and then climbs sharply to vistas of north and west. SHT follows rock promontories in a series of short ascents and descents. From ridge SHT descends steeply into valley and wetter area.

▲ BEAVER POND CAMPSITE

TYPE: regular
TENT PADS: 4
WATER: From beaver pond
SETTING: 2.0 miles east of
    Chapins Creek
PREVIOUS CAMPSITE: 2.2 miles
NEXT CAMPSITE: 1.5 miles

**HISTORY OF
SPLIT ROCK LIGHTHOUSE**

For a few centuries now, people have been trying to move safely along the North Shore of Lake Superior. Split Rock Lighthouse, which is visible from a number of points along the SHT, was one of many efforts to make the trip easier. Built in response to a particularly tragic year of shipwrecks (1905, with 215 lives lost on the lake), the lighthouse operated from 1910 to 1961. The light was visible up to 60 miles away. Today, the lighthouse is owned by the State of Minnesota and is one of the most popular tourist sites on the North Shore, with over 200,000 visitors a year.

7.1 (4.2)
FAULT LINE CREEK CAMPSITE

SHT comes to beaver pond, crosses Fault Line Creek, passes high mound of giant boulders, then follows the rocky shore of the beaver pond. SHT climbs steeply through birch forest to Fault Line Ridge, formed by a geologic fault. SHT proceeds along east rim of fault valley, with dramatic views into the deep valley.

▲ FAULT LINE CREEK CAMPSITE

TYPE: Multi-group
TENT PADS: 8
WATER: From beaver pond
SETTING: On shore of large beaver pond
PREVIOUS CAMPSITE: 1.5 miles
NEXT CAMPSITE: 4.35 miles

7.6 (3.7)
JUNCTION WITH WEST COVE POINT SPUR

At a major break in Fault Line Ridge, this spur trail leads to Cove Point on the shore (see sidebar). SHT continues along ridgeline, then after one last overlook turns east and follows cliffs above Beaver River. Views include the railroad tracks linking the taconite mines of Babbitt with the processing plant in Silver Bay. Hikers can hear, and in season see, Glen Avon Falls on the Beaver River.

9.4 (1.9)
JUNCTION WITH EAST COVE POINT SPUR

Take this spur trail 200 yards to view of Lake Superior or continue all the way down to the shore. SHT continues towards Co. Rd. 4 through birch, maple, and balsam forests, with groves of cedar in some low areas. SHT crosses a snowmobile trail 30 yards before Co. Rd. 4.

11.3 (0.0)
CO. RD. 4 PARKING LOT

COVE POINT SPUR TRAIL LOOP

This loop section was built in 1996 with assistance from volunteers provided by Cove Point Lodge. With a little less than three new miles of trail a great six-mile loop was created, including the dramatic cliffs above the Beaver River and at the Fault Line Ridge.

The SHT spur begins just above the Cove Point Lodge parking lot, crosses Highway 61 and continues uphill, crossing a stream and passing through a former mink farm. After passing a communications tower, the spur trail comes to the junction at 1.2 miles.

The eastern spur leads about a half mile through birch forest to two hills, the second with a dramatic overlook of Lake Superior and the interior. This was previously a dead end overlook of the original SHT.

The eastern spur travels on the main SHT 1.8 miles to the western spur. This section of the SHT passes the Beaver River overlook cliffs and the Fault Line Ridge overlooks with their numerous red pines.

The western spur is longer, 1.1 miles. It heads back to Cove Point from the SHT at a major break in the Fault Line Ridge. The western spur ascends a steep rocky staircase, then follows the rim of a gorge to the left. Several small rises are encountered. After crossing and following a stream the western spur meets the eastern spur at the junction back to Cove Point Lodge.

Beaver Bay to Silver Bay

START (END)
Lake Co. Rd. 4 (Lax Lake Rd.),
0.8 miles north of Beaver Bay

END (START)
Lake Co. Rd. 5 (Penn Blvd.),
north of Silver Bay

LENGTH OF TRAIL SECTION
4.7 miles

SAFETY CONCERNS
• Crossing of active Northshore
  Mining Company railroad
  tracks

• Watch trail signs closely as
  numerous other trails and
  roads intersect with SHT

ACCESS AND PARKING
Nearest Hwy. 61 milepost: 51.1

Secondary road name and
number: 0.8 miles north on
Co. Rd. 4 to parking lot on
right. Overnight okay.

FACILITIES
At starting trailhead (farthest
southwest): none

Designated campsites on this
section of SHT: two

SYNOPSIS
This section of trail follows the
lovely Beaver River with its
gorgeous falls for over a half
mile before turning away from
the river, following an old road,
and then climbing a high ridge
studded with pines. The trail
continues along the ridge with
dramatic views of the Beaver
River valley. After descending to
cross the Silver Bay Golf Course
Road, the trail again climbs to
the ridgeline with many
challenging ascents and
descents, traveling on rocky outcrops and affording stunning
views of Lake Superior.

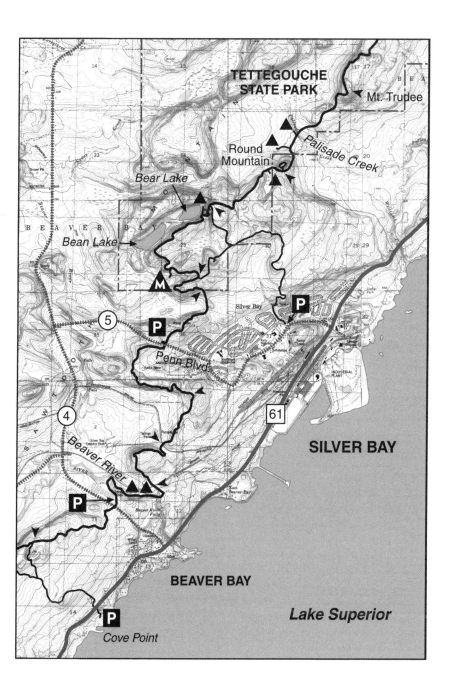

TETTEGOUCHE
STATE PARK

Mt. Trudee

Palisade Creek

Round
Mountain

Bear Lake

Bean Lake

M

P

5

Penn Blvd

4

Beaver River

RIVER

P

61

SILVER BAY

P

BEAVER BAY

Lake Superior

P

Cove Point

MILE-BY-MILE DESCRIPTION

0.0 (4.7)
LAKE CO. RD. 4 PARKING LOT

SHT leaves lot along snowmobile/ATV trail (the Silver Bay Grant-in-Aid Trail) with wide views of valley, passing by some settling ponds, and soon crosses Beaver River on a bridge shared by the SHT and snowmobiles. SHT turns right down east bank of river immediately after bridge. This scenic river walk passes groves of cedar and white pine, following the river as it changes from a gentle wide river to a roaring cascade. Near falls, SHT turns away from river and climbs through cedar, spruce, and birch to join the Betzler Rd. SHT turns left (north) on the road.

▲ NORTH BEAVER RIVER CAMPSITE

TYPE: Regular
TENT PADS: 3
WATER: From Beaver River
SETTING: 0.75 miles from Beaver River trailhead
PREVIOUS CAMPSITE: 4.35 miles
NEXT CAMPSITE: .25 miles

▲ SOUTH BEAVER RIVER CAMPSITE

TYPE: Regular
TENT PADS: 3
WATER: From Beaver River
SETTING: 1.0 miles from Beaver Bay trailhead
PREVIOUS CAMPSITE: .25 miles
NEXT CAMPSITE: 5.8 miles

MINNESOTA'S TACONITE INDUSTRY

Since the 1950s, the history and landscape of the Beaver Bay area have been tied to the processing and shipping of taconite, a low-grade iron ore found naturally in deposits 50 miles inland. Reserve Mining Company built the world's first large taconite concentrating and pelletizing plant, creating the company town of Silver Bay. In the 1970s Reserve Mining drew criticism for its practice of dumping many thousands of tons of taconite tailings into Lake Superior daily. Following a 1978 federal court ruling, Reserve built the immense Milepost 7 tailings pond a few miles behind Beaver Bay. The tailings sludge is pumped through huge pipes from the Silver Bay plant. Reserve Mining Co. closed its Babbitt mine and Silver Bay plant in 1986. In 1989, Cyprus Minerals Company bought the plant and reopened it on a smaller scale. Since 1994, NorthShore Mining has been a subsidiary of Cleveland Cliffs.

1.1 (3.6)
RAILROAD TRACKS CROSSING
SHT follows the Betzler Rd. which crosses the main line bringing taconite to Silver Bay for processing from the mine in Babbitt. SHT follows Betzler Rd. for another 100 yards, then at intersection goes due north into a balsam thicket, then up a nice, fragrant stand of red and white pines to Sulheim's Overlook, with a view of ridges, forest, and far in the distance the tailings basin. SHT continues along cliff edge with a view of tailings ponds and the pumping station.

2.2 (2.5)
GOLF COURSE RD. CROSSING
SHT comes out onto a snowmobile/ATV trail and follows it for 20 yards, crosses the Silver Bay Golf Course Road, and then follows the snowmobile/ATV trail for another 25 yards. SHT leaves the snowmobile/ATV on the right and goes uphill in a stand of aspens. SHT then leads gradually uphill to an overlook amidst red pines with views of Lake Superior. As visible from the overlook, the forest here is a sea of birches with occasional towering white and red pines. SHT continues through this forest, up a ridgeline, across an ATV trail and then up to a rocky open ridgeline.

3.2 (1.5)
VIEW OF SILVER BAY, NORTHSHORE MINING PLANT
SHT follows ridge overlooking Silver Bay. Note unusual clumps of low, leafy bearberry and juniper. SHT winds along first ridge, then descends and climbs again to a second ridge, called "Blueberry Ridge" by the locals. From a clump of red pines one can look back to the parking lot on Co. Rd. 4 where the hike began. A beaver pond below may provide an opportunity for watching beavers at work. SHT descends into mixed woods, past a trail, through a wet area with ash trees, then gently up to one final rocky ridge before crossing a snowmobile trail and crossing Penn Blvd. to parking lot.

4.7 (0.0)
PENN BLVD. TRAILHEAD AND PARKING LOT

Silver Bay to Tettegouche State Park and Highway 1

START (END)
Lake Co. Rd. 5 (Penn Blvd.), north of Silver Bay

END (START)
State Hwy. 1 (or Tettegouche State Park Trail Center)

LENGTH OF TRAIL SECTION
11.1 miles to Hwy. 1; 10.0 miles to trailhead in state park

SAFETY CONCERNS
• Trail often follows cliff edges, so use caution with small children. Steep downhills can be slippery in wet weather.

ACCESS AND PARKING
Nearest Hwy. 61 milepost: 54.3 (stoplight at Outer Drive)

Secondary road name and number: Outer Drive, take through town to the stop sign at which point the road becomes Lake Co. Rd. 5 (Penn Blvd.) and proceed 0.5 mile to parking lot on right. Overnight okay.

TWIN LAKES TRAIL OPTION
Take Outer Drive 0.5 miles from Hwy. 61 to Bay Area Historical Society parking lot on right. SHT spur leaves from far end of lot (see sidebar). Spur is also labeled "Twin Lakes Trail" (for Bean and Bear Lakes). Plenty of parking. Overnight okay with permission from Historical Society. The loop is 7.6 miles going from the Historical Society parking lot. If you hike the loop from the Penn Blvd parking lot, the loop is 6.8 miles. Note that from the Historical Society the trail begins on a rough ATV trail.

FACILITIES
At starting trailhead (farthest southwest): none

Designated campsites on this section of SHT: five

SYNOPSIS
This is one of the more challenging sections of the SHT, with lots of up and down, great views of Lake Superior and inland bluffs. It begins in the outskirts of Silver Bay and winds past beautiful Bean and Bear Lakes in Tettegouche State Park. The trail continues through Tettegouche past Round Mountain and Mt. Trudee with fantastic views and then by the backcountry "gem lakes." The highlight of the section is the dramatic High Falls on the Baptism River.

MILE-BY-MILE DESCRIPTION

0.0 (11.1)
PENN BLVD.

SHT departs parking area on snowmobile/ATV trail for 100 yards then turns left up hill. The trail crosses an ATV trail, passes a sumac stand, crosses a gravel road (to Silver Bay's water supply), and then passes under a powerline into spruce trees. SHT then ascends ridgeline and crosses another ATV trail. Green or blue paint on rocks marks SHT route, although these are not official markers.

1.0 (10.1)
SERIES OF OUTCROPS WITH SOUTH AND WEST VIEWS

Views over Silver Bay, water tower, Northshore Mining plant, and Lake Superior. View at 1.3 miles of oak-maple-birch ridge.

1.8 (9.3)
WESTERN JUNCTION WITH TWIN LAKES TRAIL

One of two junctions with the Twin Lakes Trail, also makes for a nice "lollipop loop" hike through maples. SHT crosses footbridge on Penn Creek, enters forest with maples dominating the low portion of the south-facing slope, then passes outcrops with oak and sumac. Lots of blueberries and june-

TWIN LAKES TRAIL

How about a walk through town? When the town is nestled in the wilderness like Silver Bay, that can be quite a trek. The Twin Lakes Trail, named after the dramatic Bean and Bear Lakes, is a 7.6 mile "lollipop loop" that has a "stem" of 2.3 miles before it splits apart to visit the lakes.

The trail starts at the Bay Area Historical Society parking lot in Silver Bay. Watch for the distinctive Twin Lakes Trail signs. It crosses Banks Blvd., then continues up a hill and a very nice little hogback area. After 0.7 mile watch for a spur trail on the right; it's 0.7 miles long with some nice views of the City. You'll find interesting views looking west. After crossing ATV trails, at 2.3 miles is the loop junction.

The 0.7 mile west spur leads to Elam's Knob, a lovely spot for a break, about halfway along this side plus a short climb. The east spur takes you up a rocky hillside.

The 1.6 miles of the SHT this loop contains are among the most picturesque of the whole trail. At the end, head over to the Dairy Queen. This may be one of the most scenic hikes anywhere you can end with a Peanut Buster Parfait!

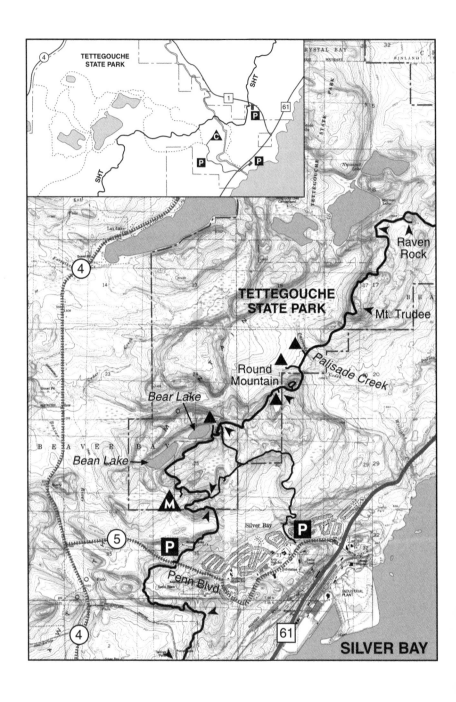

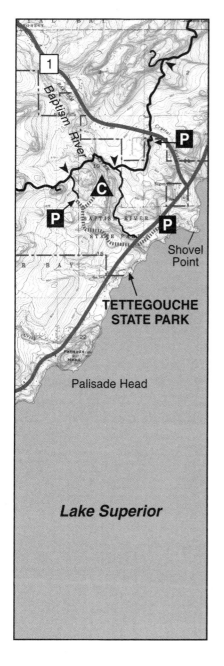

berries in this area of the SHT. At one outcrop you can see back to the previous outcrop and a beaver pond before SHT descends.

⚠ PENN CREEK CAMPSITE

TYPE: Multi-group
TENT PADS: 8
WATER: From Penn Creek
SETTING: 2.0 miles east of
  Penn Blvd.
PREVIOUS CAMPSITE: 5.8 miles
NEXT CAMPSITE: 1.4 miles

2.6 (8.5)
BEAN LAKE OVERLOOK

From overlook Mt. Trudee is visible to the east, marked by dark red pines and a flat top. SHT travels the length of Bean and Bear Lakes on high cliffs looking down on the sparkling lakes far below.

3.4 (7.7)
BEAR LAKE CAMPSITE

The 150-yard spur trail to the campsite at Bear Lake is on the left and descends sharply to the lake.

▲ BEAR LAKE CAMPSITE

TYPE: Regular
TENT PADS: 4
WATER: From Bear Lake
SETTING: 3.4 miles east of
  Penn Blvd., 150 yards off SHT
  on spur, on NE corner of
  Bear Lake
PREVIOUS CAMPSITE: 1.4 miles
NEXT CAMPSITE: 1.2 miles

3.6 (7.5)
EASTERN JUNCTION WITH TWIN LAKES TRAIL

At top of bluff, find the next junction with Twin Lakes Trail marked with a sign. SHT goes through level maple-birch woods, drops to an overlook of valley and view of Round Mountain and Mt. Trudee and descends to beaver pond.

▲ ROUND MOUNTAIN BEAVER POND CAMPSITE

TYPE: Regular
TENT PADS: 6
WATER: From beaver pond
SETTING: 0.1 miles west of Round Mountain spur
PREVIOUS CAMPSITE: 1.2 miles
NEXT CAMPSITE: 0.8 miles

4.8 (6.3)
SPUR TRAIL UP ROUND MOUNTAIN

0.25-mile spur trail to dramatic overlook of the expansive Palisade Creek Valley. SHT passes mature sugar maple forest and descends into Palisade Creek Valley, crossing ATV trail, two foot bridges and a wet area with white cedars. SHT crosses West Palisade Creek. 300-yard spur trail to campsite. SHT then passes East Palisade Creek campsite and descends to 25-foot bridge over East Palisade Creek. SHT crosses ATV trail, climbs a series of wooden steps through mixed woods to stunning views.

▲ WEST PALISADE CREEK CAMPSITE

TYPE: Regular
TENT PADS: 5
WATER: From West Palisade Creek
SETTING: 1.0 miles west of Mt. Trudee
PREVIOUS CAMPSITE: 0.8 miles
NEXT CAMPSITE: 0.2 miles

▲ EAST PALISADE CREEK CAMPSITE

TYPE: Regular
TENT PADS: 4
WATER: From East Palisade Creek
SETTING: 0.8 miles west of Mt. Trudee
PREVIOUS CAMPSITE: 0.2 miles
NEXT CAMPSITE: 7.8 miles (or use Tettegouche State Park)

6.3 (4.8)
MT. TRUDEE

Mt. Trudee offers one of the SHT's best examples of a large, weather-resistant anorthosite dome. Its summit is picturesque, studded with pines, with great views. SHT continues along top of Trudee, with views including Tettegouche and Mic Mac Lakes (named after lakes in Labrador, Canada), then descends through maple forest. Forest changes to mixed maple-birch, starting at a series of rock walls alongside SHT. There is a short spur to a view of Mt. Trudee and the Palisade Valley. This was the area proposed by Reserve Mining to fill with taconite tailings.

7.5 (3.6)
JUNCTION WITH STATE PARK TRAIL

Park post with letter "L." State park trail goes 1.0 miles to Tettegouche Camp and Conservancy Pines. SHT continues on state park trail, first through pure maples, past mileage sign, and over a 40-foot plank bridge, then through low area and a copse of white cedars. A spur trail leads to good views from Raven Rock.

TETTEGOUCHE STATE PARK

Tettegouche State Park was established in 1979, and contains 9,346 acres of land, including six inland lakes and one mile of Lake Superior shoreline. Flowing through the park is the Baptism River and on it, High Falls, the highest falls completely in Minnesota. At the southeast corner of the park lies Palisade Head, a high bluff with a sheer rock face falling 200 feet into Lake Superior below. The park has 34 campsites. The rugged, semi-mountainous terrain, and spectacular overlooks, make hiking on the park's seventeen miles of trails very popular. A one-mile self-guided trail to Shovel Point along Lake Superior educates as well as inspires. For the history buff, there is the Tettegouche Camp, a 1910 social camp. Its log buildings have been restored for overnight rentals. In addition, there is rich logging, maple syruping, and mining history throughout the park.

8.2 (2.9)
JUNCTION WITH STATE PARK TRAIL

Park post with letter "C." Tricky spot on maps. SHT descends through mixed maple-birch-conifer forest, past a 12-foot circumference white

WOLF RIDGE ENVIRONMENTAL LEARNING CENTER

The Wolf Ridge Environmental Learning Center (WRELC) facility is a cluster of buildings with 1000 acres of surrounding land which accommodates hundreds of students, both youth and adult. Wolf Ridge has been at its current site since 1988, though the program started in Isabella, Minnesota, in the early 1970s. The well-regarded residential environmental education program has introduced over a quarter-million students to the wonders of the north woods; weekend programs offer a wide variety of experiences for adults and families. The trails on the WRELC intersect with the SHT, allowing for excursions onto the SHT from the WRELC parking lot. Look for the Wolf Ridge turnoff a few miles up Lake Co. Rd. 6.

pine, then through "The Drainpipe," a 150-foot rock crevice with rock steps. SHT emerges into dominant birch stand being replaced by the spruce and balsam fir understory. SHT crosses another ski trail and leads through white cedar lowland. Look for spur trail up to view of Lake Superior and Palisade valley.

9.7 (1.4)
JUNCTION WITH ACCESS TRAIL TO TETTEGOUCHE STATE PARK TRAILHEAD PARKING LOT

Park post with letter "B." To access Tettegouche parking lot, turn on ski trail. Go 0.3 miles downhill to parking lot, through a white pine grove, passing state park post "A." Main SHT continues through mature birch, across plank walkways. Watch for spur trail to state park campground. Main SHT descends wooden stairs past Baptism High Falls overlook, then crosses Baptism River on suspension bridge just above the falls. These are the highest falls entirely in Minnesota. The bridge, built in 1991 with substantial help from Minnesota Power, has a unique single-cable suspension design. This was by far the most elaborate and expensive bridge built by the SHTA. At trailside bench on other side of river, look for spur trail to base of High Falls. SHT leaves river and goes up wood staircase.

10.4 (0.7)
JUNCTION WITH STATE PARK TRAIL

Spur trail follows river downstream 1.3 miles to park visitor center and wayside rest. The main SHT goes into birch woods and across a narrow roadbed. Two large white pines on the side, followed by a balsam fir "tunnel" for 200 yards. SHT leads through cedars, up a hill and along a ridge, then climbs 100-yard rock staircase. The large rock amphitheater is a former quarry site, the first quarry used in the early days of the 3M Company. Spur leads to SHT parking lot off Hwy. 1.

11.1 (0.0)
STATE HWY. 1 TRAILHEAD PARKING LOT

SUGAR MAPLE FORESTS

The extensive maple forests of the SHT, which create much of the gorgeous colors of a fall hike, are the result of a lucky combination of ecological factors. Sugar maples require relatively warm winters and fairly deep soil to survive, both of which are rare in northern Minnesota. Maples can't survive below -40 °. The thermal mass of Lake Superior keeps the north shore cool in the summer, but also keeps the area warm in winter. Maples thrive on the ridgelines, but not in the adjacent valleys, into which cold air sinks. The maple forests get their deep soil as a gift from two different glaciers which advanced parallel to each other, on both sides of the ridgeline, leaving enough glacial till on the ridges for this beautiful, out-of-place forest to thrive.

Highway 1 to Lake County Road 6

START (END)
State Hwy. 1, 0.8 miles north of Illgen City

END (START)
Lake Co. Rd. 6 (Little Marais Rd.), north of Little Marais

LENGTH OF TRAIL SECTION
6.8 miles

SAFETY CONCERNS
• On several sections the SHT runs along the edges of cliffs

• Steep sections of trail slippery when wet

ACCESS AND PARKING
Nearest Hwy. 61 milepost: 59.3

Secondary road name and number: Hwy. 1

Go north on Hwy. 1 0.8 miles. Parking lot on left, marked with small sign. Space for 6 cars. Overnight okay.

FACILITIES
At starting trailhead (farthest southwest): none

Designated campsites on this section of SHT: two

SYNOPSIS
This section, one of the most challenging, varies greatly from easy, long stretches along the contours to steep, scrambling ascents and descents. There are many open ledges affording beautiful views of both Lake Superior and its shoreline, and inland lakes, mountains and valleys. The trail winds through pockets of maples.

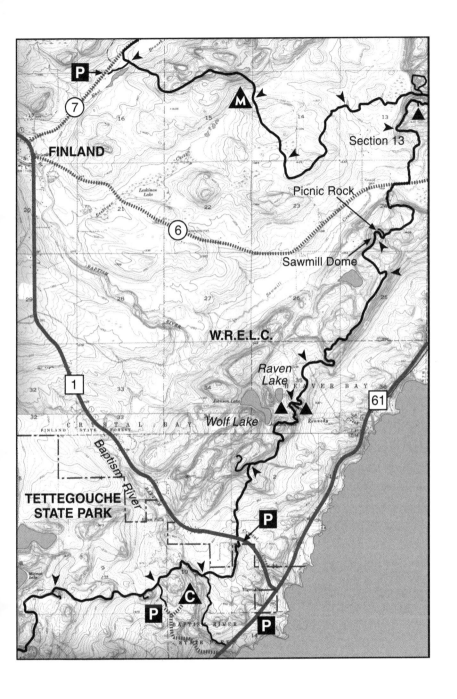

FINLAND

Section 13

Picnic Rock

Sawmill Dome

W.R.E.L.C.

Raven
Lake

Wolf Lake

TETTEGOUCHE
STATE PARK

MILE-BY-MILE DESCRIPTION

0.0 (6.8)
STATE HWY. 1
SHT crosses Crystal Creek and enters a 1990 burned area of birch and aspen, marked with a sign. SHT crosses gravel logging road and traverses wet area. Note Sawtooth summits ahead. SHT soon climbs steeply toward these summits.

0.9 (5.9)
SPUR TRAIL TO FANTASIA OVERLOOK
0.5-mile spur trail with views of Lake Superior, Palisade Head, Mt. Trudee, and the Silver Bay Harbor. Below are views of vertical cliffs and a beaver pond. The main SHT continues downhill from the overlook trail, levels out in a valley where it briefly shares an old road, then rises sharply to open ledges with view of Lake Superior. SHT turns away from the lake, drops a bit, and then climbs switchbacks to an overlook above Wolf Lake, a beautiful lake deep in a depression, originally known as Johnson Lake. From the overlook, SHT curves around the peak, descends, then climbs again to a ridgeline overlooking Lake Superior.

2.3 (4.5)
KENNEDY CREEK CAMPSITES
SHT heads back into the woods to West Kennedy Creek Campsite. SHT continues across bridge, past spur trail that leads inland to Wolf Ridge Environmental Learning Center. SHT climbs to a small dome. From the dome, SHT descends again.

▲ WEST KENNEDY CREEK CAMPSITE

TYPE: Regular
TENT PADS: 5
WATER: From Kennedy Creek
SETTING: 2.3 miles east of Hwy. 1, within Wolf Ridge ELC boundaries
PREVIOUS CAMPSITE: 7.8 miles
NEXT CAMPSITE: 0.1 miles

▲ EAST KENNEDY CREEK CAMPSITE

TYPE: Regular
TENT PADS: 4
WATER: From Kennedy Creek
SETTING: 2.4 miles east of Hwy. 1
PREVIOUS CAMPSITE: 0.1 miles
NEXT CAMPSITE: 5.8 miles

2.9 (3.9)
POWERLINE
100 yards before powerline, SHT crosses old Johnson Lake Rd., also XC trail leading to Wolf Ridge. SHT continues and climbs to an expansive view of Lake Superior, Fantasia, Mystical Mountain and Marshall Mountain. SHT follows a curving cliff line before it parallels the lake on a high ridge, with fleeting glimpses of Lake Superior. The trail passes through two big rocks.

4.7 (2.1)
OVERLOOK
From the overlook, SHT turns sharply inland towards Sawmill Dome, and remains level through maple woods until a last rise to the top of Sawmill Dome. This large cliff is studded with large pines and overlooks a maple forest, farmsteads, and buildings of Wolf Ridge ELC. Sawmill Dome and Sawmill Creek in the valley below are named after the turn-of-the-century Warren Sawmill in Little Marais.

6.0 (0.8)
SAWMILL DOME
SHT skirts Sawmill Dome with steep cliffs, then descends sharply, past a spur trail to Picnic Rock, which goes 150 yards to a semi-cave at base of cliffs. SHT continues to an overlook of Sawmill Creek valley, old Air Force radar base, and Co. Rd. 6, then descends. The trail climbs briefly up log and rock steps to a hilltop with views of Lake Superior and ridgeline. It then descends past stone steps and wildlife opening.

6.8 (0.0)
LAKE CO. RD. 6 (LITTLE MARAIS RD.)
Parking lot is 0.4 miles east on Co. Rd. 6, in gravel pit. SHT continues on other side of road after entry onto Co. Rd. 6 and before parking lot.

Lake County Road 6 to Finland Recreation Center

START (END)
Lake Co. Rd. 6 (Little Marais Rd.), north of Little Marais

END (START)
Finland Recreation Center, 1.3 miles east of Finland on Lake Co. Rd. 7 (Cramer Rd.)

LENGTH OF TRAIL SECTION
7.6 miles

SAFETY CONCERNS
• Cliffs at Section 13

• Boardwalk at beaver dam

• Watch closely for trail markers where SHT crosses logging roads

ACCESS AND PARKING
Nearest Hwy. 61 milepost: 65.3

Secondary road name: Lake Co. Rd. 6 (Little Marais Road)

Go 2.1 miles on Lake Co. Rd. 6 to parking lot on right in gravel pit. Trailhead is 0.2 miles west on Co. Rd. 6. Many parking spaces available in front part of gravel pit. Overnight okay.

FACILITIES
At starting trailhead: none

Designated campsites on this section of SHT: two

SYNOPSIS
This hike leads to some of the most impressive terrain on the SHT, including the high cliffs overlooking the Sawmill Creek and Baptism River valleys, popular with local rock climbers and known as the Section 13 cliffs. There is an impressive boardwalk that has been constructed over a beaver dam and a huge rock, known as a glacial erratic, that is over 20 feet tall. This section passes through excellent moose habitat. The hike ends with a trek through a valley that includes the east branch of the Baptism River.

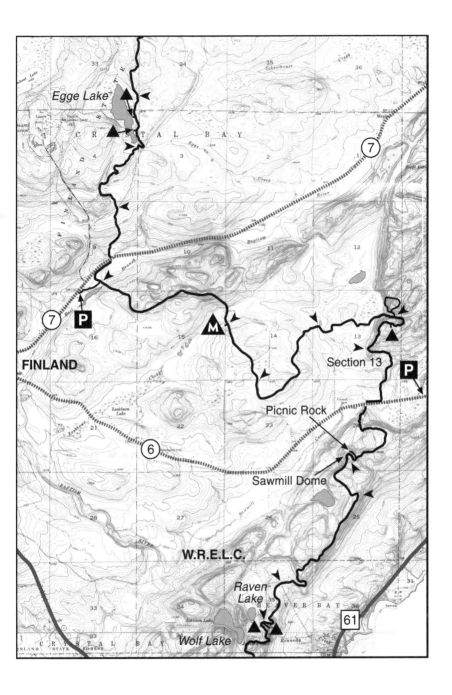

Egge Lake

C R I S T A L   B A Y

⑦

⑦   P

FINLAND

M

Section 13

P

Picnic Rock

6

Sawmill Dome

W.R.E.L.C.

Raven Lake

Wolf Lake

61

MILE-BY-MILE DESCRIPTION

0.0 (7.6)
LAKE CO. RD. 6 (LITTLE MARAIS RD.)

SHT departs from Co. Rd. 6 about 0.2 miles west of parking lot.
SHT enters dark spruce and birch forest, then crosses corduroy boardwalk through wet areas. SHT crosses Sawmill Creek and then another
small creek. SHT climbs gradually along a fir- and spruce-lined ridge,
past a beaver pond. At first there are scattered maples, but as the SHT
climbs, the maples dominate. SHT climbs steeply.

1.0 (6.6)
FIRST OUTCROP/VIEW

The first view of the valley occurs here. SHT continues up rocky
ridgeline. Note the occasional oak trees, a sign of drier microclimates
on the ridgelines. In late fall, look for Lake Superior views. A little
further up, follow short spur to another dramatic view. The widest
view comes at the open rocky ridge, a common rock-climbing area
known as "Section 13." Spectacular views from here of steep rock
cliffs, inland ridges, beaver pond, and the old Finland radar base. SHT
continues to another rock outcrop (again, with seasonal Lake Superior
views), then descends into a cedar-filled gulch.

▲ SECTION 13 CAMPSITE

TYPE: Regular
TENT PADS: 4
WATER: No water source—get water south of campsite at
   Sawmill Creek or 0.5 miles north of campsite from
   small creek
SETTING: 1.4 miles from Co. Rd. 6
PREVIOUS CAMPSITE: 5.8 miles
NEXT CAMPSITE: 3.8 miles

1.8 (5.8)
SPUR TO OVERLOOK

The 0.8-mile spur loop climbs to views of cliffs, then runs above valley to another set of views from a rocky, red pine ridge, before looping
back. SHT descends through cedars along an unnamed creek, then
crosses it. Watch footing on descent. Section 13 cliffs tower above the

trees. SHT travels through mixed forest over low-lying areas with short boardwalks. SHT continues to large beaver pond.

3.0 (4.6)
BOARDWALK AT BEAVER DAM
SHT crosses 440 feet of boardwalk over dam. There is a bench on the west side, good for a lunch spot. SHT ascends through a logged area. Look south here for a great view of the Section 13 hills. SHT continues through open area, then enters mixed forest and passes by a huge rock, called a glacial erratic. SHT enters planted area. Watch out for cross trails. Lots of wildflowers blooming in season. SHT leaves plantation area on northeast side and descends through mixed forest to Park Hill Road.

4.4 (3.2)
PARK HILL ROAD
No parking here. SHT enters bog area with long boardwalks to protect it from foot traffic. Look closely and you might see a lady slipper. SHT moves through deciduous forest, across old logging road and descends to Leskinen Campsite and Creek.

▲ LESKINEN CREEK CAMPSITE

TYPE: Multi-group
TENT PADS: 8
WATER: from Leskinen Creek
SETTING: 0.8 miles north of Park Hill Rd.
PREVIOUS CAMPSITE: 3.8 miles
NEXT CAMPSITE: 4.7 miles

5.2 (2.4)
LESKINEN CREEK
SHT climbs gradually away from creek through mixed forest, then climbs more steeply to top of ridge. SHT descends from ridge, then up to second ridge with views to the southeast toward Sawmill Dome and Lake Superior. SHT descends to Finland Ski Trail and follows it downhill. Watch for signs. SHT descends to East Branch of Baptism River. Bridge here is shared with the ski trail. SHT goes north along Tower Creek for 0.1 miles to junction with spur trail to Finland Recreation Center parking lot. Watch for fish ramp at bridge over Tower Creek.

PROTECTING EGGE LAKE

The next section of SHT includes beautiful Egge Lake.

The rolling landscape of Egge Lake is part of a 700-acre parcel that was privately owned until 1999. The Nature Conservancy of Minnesota had an option to buy it, but offered this option to the Parks and Trails Council of Minnesota. The Council is a non-profit group that, according to its mission statement, "acts to help establish, develop and enhance Minnesota's parks and trails, and to encourage their protection and enjoyment."
The Council bought the land, to swap for land owned by Lake County but held within the boundary of Crosby Manitou State Park. The Egge Lake parcel is to become county forest, and the park's holdings will get bigger.

The end result is that this beautiful tract of northern hardwood forest will be preserved within a larger county forest management scheme. Left to private ownership, this inland lake could have been developed with roads and cabins. Collaboration between businesses, non-profit groups and government saved the day.

7.3 (0.3)
JUNCTION WITH SPUR TRAIL

Spur goes 0.3 miles southwest through mixed forest to Finland Recreation Center parking lot. Main SHT continues 0.1 miles to Co. Rd. 7 and then northeast 0.2 miles on Co. Rd. 7 to reach next trail section.

7.6 (0.0)
FINLAND RECREATION CENTER TRAILHEAD PARKING LOT

Finland Recreation Center to Crosby-Manitou State Park

START (END)
Finland Recreation Center, 1.3 miles east of Finland on Lake Co. Rd. 7 (Cramer Rd.)

END (START)
Crosby-Manitou State Park

LENGTH OF TRAIL SECTION
11.8 miles to Crosby-Manitou State Park

7.5 miles to Sonju Lake parking lot

SAFETY CONCERNS
• Intersections with snowmobile trail

ACCESS AND PARKING
Nearest Hwy. 61 milepost: 59.3

Secondary road name and number: Hwy. 1 and Lake Co. Rd. 7 (Cramer Rd.)

From Hwy. 61 go 7.4 miles north on Hwy. 1 to junction with Co. Rd. 7 (Cramer Rd.). Turn right on Co. Rd. 7. Go 1.3 miles to parking lot past ball field at Finland Recreation Center. Overnight okay.

FACILITIES
At starting trailhead: outhouses at parking lot

Designated campsites on this section of the SHT: seven

SYNOPSIS
This section, while longer, is relatively level hiking. It offers a wide variety of terrain and forest types. SHT passes through beautiful maple forests, groves of large cedar, excellent moose habitat and two spectacular inland lakes. Unique features of this section are the old trapper's cabin and the boardwalk to the island on Sonju Lake.

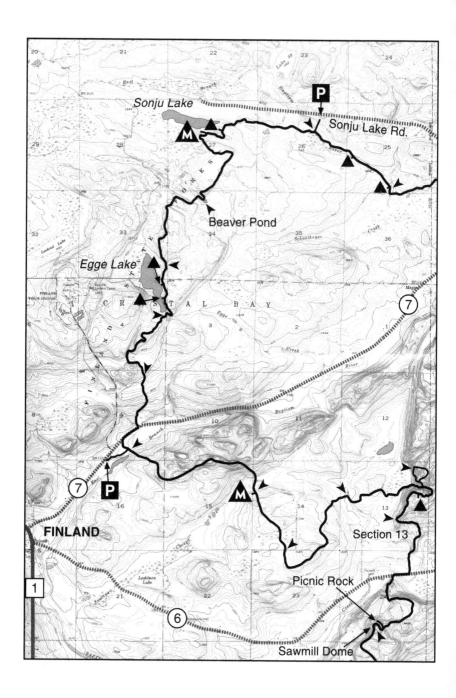

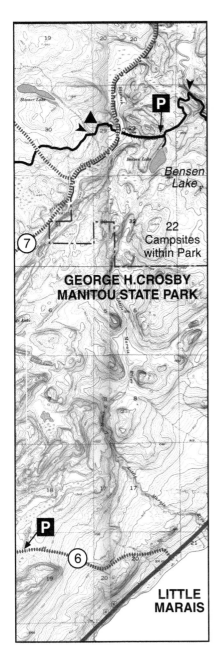

7

GEORGE H.CROSBY MANITOU STATE PARK

Bensen Lake

22 Campsites within Park

6

LITTLE MARAIS

MILE-BY-MILE DESCRIPTION

0.0 (11.8)
PARKING LOT
From the parking lot, a 0.3-mile spur leads to the main SHT. SHT reaches Co. Rd. 7 and follows the road for 0.2 miles then enters a hardwood forest dominated by maples and climbs. SHT crosses an old logging road before coming to North Shore State Trail.

1.1 (10.7)
NORTH SHORE STATE TRAIL
SHT crosses the North Shore State Trail, route of the John Beargrease Sled Dog Marathon each winter, and continues through mixed forest of birch, balsam fir and cedar. SHT follows over 200 feet of boardwalk, then continues gentle ascent. SHT crosses unnamed creek and climbs gently. The forest becomes predominantly maple.

2.3 (9.5)
EGGE LAKE
SHT reaches Egge Lake, then follows Egge Creek steeply downhill. SHT crosses the creek over a scenic gorge, then doubles back toward Egge Lake. SHT continues along ridge above Egge Lake. After the South and North Egge Lake campsites,

SHT passes under tree that forms a natural arch and continues through a maple forest.

▲ SOUTH EGGE LAKE CAMPSITE

TYPE: Regular
TENT PADS: 4
WATER: From Egge Lake
SETTING: On lake shore with view of opposite shore
PREVIOUS CAMPSITE: 4.7 miles
NEXT CAMPSITE: 0.2 miles

▲ NORTH EGGE LAKE CAMPSITE

TYPE: Regular
TENT PADS: 4
WATER: From Egge Lake
SETTING: On lake shore
PREVIOUS CAMPSITE: 0.2 miles
NEXT CAMPSITE: 3.1 miles

3.0 (8.8)
OLD TRAPPER'S CABIN

SHT passes by an old trapper's cabin. This is a unique historical feature—please use care when observing so as not to disturb or harm the site. Watch out for broken glass on the ground. After leaving the cabin, SHT enters a cedar grove. Observe the numbers on the trees; this was most likely a study site in the past. SHT passes a natural rock ledge bench, then turns and climbs away from Egge Lake, descends into a ravine, then climbs again.

4.4 (7.4)
BEAVER POND

SHT crosses boardwalk over beaver pond and follows around the pond. The beaver lodge is visible at a turn in the trail. SHT ascends from beaver pond through alternating cedar and maple forests.

5.9 (5.9)
SOUTH SONJU LAKE CAMPSITE

SHT turns onto a ridge that overlooks Sonju Lake, then descends to the lake shore. An 80-foot boardwalk leads to a small island with a view to the end of the lake.

⛺ SOUTH SONJU LAKE CAMPSITE

TYPE: Multi-Group
TENT PADS: 6
WATER: From Sonju Lake
SETTING: 200 feet from lake shore
PREVIOUS CAMPSITE: 3.1 miles
NEXT CAMPSITE: 0.3 miles

▲ NORTH SONJU LAKE CAMPSITE

TYPE: Regular
TENT PADS: 4
WATER: From Sonju Lake—dock allows easy access to water
SETTING: On lake shore
PREVIOUS CAMPSITE: 0.3 miles
NEXT CAMPSITE: 1.9 miles

6.2 (5.6)
SONJU CREEK

After crossing Sonju Creek, SHT leaves cedar grove and enters logged area with immature spruce and planted red pine, then descends to an 80-foot boardwalk, enters a cedar forest, then comes to an open, rocky area with a valley below. The valley is prime moose habitat. Next, SHT crosses a logging road into a spruce plantation.

7.5 (4.3)
EAST BRANCH BAPTISM RIVER CROSSING

SHT crosses the river and continues downstream. To the left is a spur trail to a parking lot on Sonju Lake Rd. SHT continues along river bank.

▲ EAST BRANCH BAPTISM RIVER CAMPSITE

TYPE: Regular
TENT PADS: 4
WATER: From river
SETTING: On river bank
PREVIOUS CAMPSITE: 1.9 miles
NEXT CAMPSITE: 0.6 miles

8.7 (3.1)
BLESNER CREEK

Blesner Creek flows from Blesner Lake, named for an early 20th century homesteader. Blesner Creek enters the East Branch of the Baptism River in a cedar grove. SHT again crosses the North Shore State Trail next to a bridge across the river and soon heads away from the river through a mixed forest including a large cedar grove before crossing Sonju Lake Rd.

▲ BLESNER CREEK CAMPSITE

TYPE: Regular
TENT PADS: 3
WATER: From river or creek
SETTING: In cedar grove at intersection of creek and river
PREVIOUS CAMPSITE: 0.6 miles
NEXT CAMPSITE: 2.1 miles

10.6 (1.2)
BLESNER LAKE ROAD

SHT crosses Blesner Lake Road and passes Aspen Knob campsite. SHT climbs to a knoll overlooking the Baptism River valley before descending to Co. Rd. 7. SHT crosses the road and follows the entrance road to Crosby-Manitou State Park.

▲ ASPEN KNOB CAMPSITE

TYPE: Regular
TENT PADS: 2
WATER: From unnamed creek 300 feet away on SHT
SETTING: On a knob adjacent to the SHT
PREVIOUS CAMPSITE: 2.1 miles
NEXT CAMPSITE: 5.1 miles

11.8 (0.0)
CROSBY-MANITOU STATE PARK TRAILHEAD

Crosby-Manitou State Park to Caribou River Wayside

START (END)
Crosby-Manitou State Park, off Lake Co. Rd. 7 (Cramer Rd.)

END (START)
Caribou River State Wayside, on Hwy. 61

LENGTH OF TRAIL SECTION
8.0 miles

SAFETY CONCERNS
• Rock strewn parts of trail
• Steep descents and ascents

ACCESS AND PARKING
Nearest Hwy. 61 milepost: either 59.3 for Hwy. 1 or 65.3 for Lake Co. Rd. 6

Secondary road name and number: follow either road to Finland and continue north on Hwy. 1 past the junction with Co. Rd. 6. Turn right onto Co. Rd. 7, 8 miles to the entrance of Crosby-Manitou State Park (state park permit required). Overnight okay.

FACILITIES
At starting trailhead (farthest southwest): outhouses

Designated campsites on this section of the SHT: 22 in Crosby-Manitou State Park (requires registration and fee); sites 3 and 4 in park are on SHT; two on SHT outside of park

Note: the self-registration board is on the west side of the park. If you're hiking from the east and want to camp in the park, you either have to hike to this board or make a reservation in advance.

SYNOPSIS
This section of the SHT is quite dramatic in terms of topography, offering broad views of both inland ridges, ponds, and rivers, and of Lake Superior. The SHT here is more rugged than most sections and visits a variety of forest habitats. The western half of the section skirts the valley of the wild Manitou River, while the eastern half explores the cedar groves of the Little Manitou drainage and the dramatic Caribou River gorge.

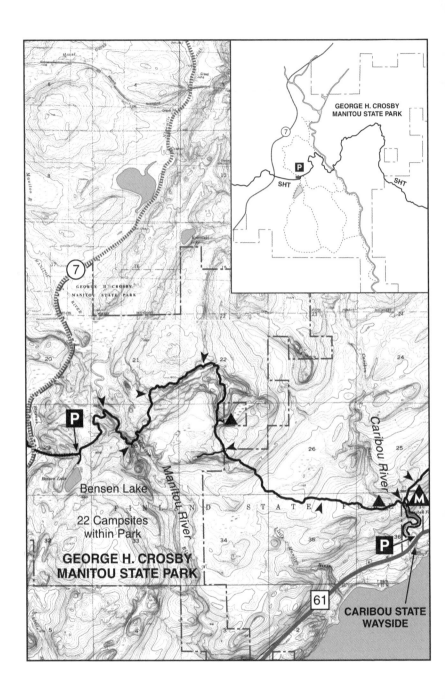

MILE-BY-MILE DESCRIPTION

0.0 (8.0)
PARKING LOT
SHT leaves from parking lot at mapboard on the "Middle Trail," travels through birch forest, past a large glacial erratic and across plank bridges. A spur on right side leads 70 yards to view of Lake Superior and Manitou River valley. SHT descends steeply through cedars.

0.9 (7.1)
JUNCTION OF SHT/MIDDLE TRAIL WITH RIVER TRAIL
Upriver from this junction about 0.25 miles are the Manitou Cascades, a worthy side trip. At junction, SHT goes downriver (right), past state park campsites 3 and 4, and up and over two bluffs with partial overlooks of river valley. Signpost marks where SHT goes steeply downhill to the Manitou River bridge, descending through a dark spruce forest and an overlook trail 100 yards before the river and bridge. The overlook allows glimpses through the forest of the tumbling river as it descends toward the bridge.

1.6 (6.4)
BRIDGE OVER MANITOU RIVER
The Manitou River is one of the most rugged river valleys along the North Shore. SHT travels past white pine on east side of valley, then into scrubby mixed woods of fir, birch, and aspen. The climb is just 600 yards long but 300 feet up. SHT passes a series of four overlooks with views of Lake Superior and the Manitou River valley.

2.3 (5.7)
VIEW OF POND
After climbing short rocky slope, view pond and birch/balsam hill behind it. Look for a variety of lichens growing on the rock. Next overlook includes Lake Superior and old Air Force radar base near Finland (white buildings). SHT continues along hilltop, alternating between maple woods and stunning views of Lake Superior. Note juneberry trees and sumac at the rocky openings. Beaver ponds are visible below. SHT eventually descends again into a deep fault line valley.

GEORGE H. CROSBY-MANITOU STATE PARK

George H. Crosby-Manitou State Park is known for its rugged beauty and fine fishing. The wild and scenic Manitou River runs through the park on its descent to Lake Superior. George Crosby, an early mining magnate, donated the property for use as a state park with the provision that development be limited. With his wishes in mind, the first backpack-only park was designed. Today visitors camp at one of many remote backpack sites located mainly along the river. Hikers self-register for sites at the camping registration board. There are 23 miles of trails in this 6,682 acre park, and fishing—especially for trout along the river or on Benson Lake—is among the most popular park uses. Because of the relatively undisturbed nature of the park it is common to encounter a variety of wildlife, such as deer and moose, or less frequently, timber wolf, vole, mink, and pileated woodpecker.

3.4 (4.6)
STREAM CROSSING SMALL BEAVER DAM

SHT then climbs away from river through balsam, birch, and cedar. Forest changes over to maple, then birch and spruce. A series of overlooks of the Little Manitou, the Finland radar base, and spectacular maple hillsides. This area is known as "Horseshoe Ridge." Rock underfoot changes to crumbly lava gravel. SHT passes cedar and white pine. Spur near small footbridge goes 70 feet to campsite.

▲ HORSESHOE RIDGE CAMPSITE

TYPE: Regular
TENT PADS: 2
WATER: From small creek just east of campsite
SETTING: 4.0 miles from Crosby-Manitou parking lot, on ridge overlooking Manitou River Valley
PREVIOUS CAMPSITE: 5.1 miles (or use Crosby-Manitou State Park campsites)
NEXT CAMPSITE: 3.1 miles

4.7 (3.3)
SPUR TO OVERLOOK

Spur leads 500 yards to wide view of Manitou, Little Manitou drainages, Lake Superior, and ridges. SHT leads to another expansive view. Look for oaks on this long, rocky ridge. After descending and another view, SHT continues through cedar swamp with plank walkways. Look for logged-over open area—a good spot for birdwatching.

6.2 (1.8)
LOGGING ROAD

Road built by Bob Silver for selectively cutting cedar in this area. SHT moves into birch/balsam woods, then a small rock outcrop and through spruces and bracken ferns. Between the logging road and the Caribou River, the SHT crosses the historic Pork Bay Trail, a Native American and voyageur trail that led from Pork Bay nine miles inland to Nine-Mile Lake. Listen for the Caribou River as the SHT descends. At the river the SHT turns left, upriver. Spur trails descend both sides of river to Hwy. 61.

▲ WEST CARIBOU RIVER CAMPSITE

TYPE: Regular
TENT PADS: 4
WATER: From Caribou River
SETTING: 1.0 miles from
    Caribou Wayside parking
PREVIOUS CAMPSITE:
    3.1 miles
NEXT CAMPSITE: 0.3 miles

BRIDGES ON THE SUPERIOR HIKING TRAIL

Some of the trail's most remarkable construction involves bridgework. Each stream that crosses the SHT is bridged, so hikers don't have to get wet or ford rivers. Approximately 40 bridges of various lengths, materials, and construction link embankments and landscapes. Although bridges are vital to trail layout, the best crossing is not always the most convenient place to build. A volunteer crew can make small wooden walkways from nearby resources, but some bridges are elaborately designed and need the transport of considerable lumber and other materials. The Baptism River suspension bridge, for example, required helicopter transport of supplies because of its complexity and location. Some bridges, like the one at Lake Agnes, were made during the winter, when larger timbers could be dragged across the ice.

7.3 (0.7)
BRIDGE OVER CARIBOU RIVER

Trail junction on east side of bridge. Main SHT continues upstream (left) after bridge. Spur runs downstream to Caribou Falls and Hwy. 61 parking lot. Along spur trail, keep an eye on river as it cascades through narrow stone walls. Sign marks where spur trail forks, spur going on narrow path down to gorgeous falls, the other spur going straight to Hwy. 61 along top of bluff. Listen for the falls if you get confused.

8.0 (0.0)
CARIBOU WAYSIDE (HWY. 61)

Caribou River Wayside to Cook County Road 1

START (END)
Caribou River State Wayside on Hwy. 61

END (START)
Cook Co. Rd. 1 (Cramer Rd.)

LENGTH OF TRAIL SECTION
9.0 miles

SAFETY CONCERNS
• Active railroad tracks

ACCESS AND PARKING
Nearest Hwy. 61 milepost: 70.5

Secondary road name and number: none

Parking lot is on north side of highway. Space for 10 cars. No overnight parking allowed at state wayside.

FACILITIES
At starting trailhead (farthest southwest): none

Designated campsites on this section of the SHT: four

SYNOPSIS
After ascending the beautiful and dramatic Caribou River gorge, this section of the SHT follows a series of ridges and overlooks through mixed forest, including one of the most beautiful pure birch stands on the trail. The bog vegetation of the Alfred's Pond area is a quiet highlight. Although this section is lengthy, it is one of the easier sections to hike—perfect for a long nature walk, with an abundance of wildflowers.

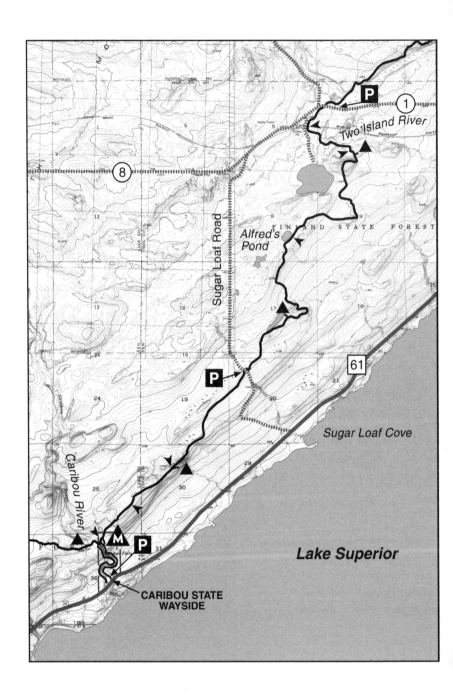

P
Two Island River
1
8
Sugar Loaf Road
Alfred's
Pond
FINLAND STATE FOREST
P
61
Sugar Loaf Cove
Caribou River
Lake Superior
M
P
CARIBOU STATE
WAYSIDE

MILE-BY-MILE DESCRIPTION

0.0 (9.0)
PARKING LOT OFF HWY. 61

There are two spur trails that connect with the SHT above Caribou Falls. West Spur Trail: Leaves from south end of Caribou River Wayside parking lot and crosses river on Hwy. 61. Spur climbs to ridge above eroded bank, descends to riverside, then gradually climbs to view of falls at ridge level. Trail continues along river gorge to junction with main SHT. East Spur Trail: Leaves from north end of parking lot. Short spur to base of Caribou Falls at .5 miles. The east spur continues along gorge of Caribou River through pine and spruce to junction with main trail.

0.7 (8.3)
JUNCTION WITH MAIN SHT

Note bridge across Caribou River. Short spur trail to campsite. Past campsite, main SHT follows small stream, then through a past logging area.

▲ EAST CARIBOU RIVER CAMPSITE

TYPE: Multi-group
TENT PADS: 10
WATER: From Caribou River
SETTING: 0.7 mile from Caribou Wayside parking lot, near the
  Caribou River bridge crossing
PREVIOUS CAMPSITE: 0.3 mile
NEXT CAMPSITE: 1.2 miles

1.2 (7.8)
LOGGING ROAD

Look carefully for SHT sign across road. Good view of Lake Superior. SHT follows ridge, along logging road and then re-enters mixed hardwoods and beautiful birch forest after powerline, with seasonal view of Lake.

2.0 (7.0)
SPUR TO CAMPSITE

Right after campsite spur trail, SHT crosses Crystal Creek on a covered bridge, then continues through marvelous birch forest. If you want, follow Crystal Creek down a ways to a collapsed mine shaft. At this mine, note the wide band of calcite crystals in the bottom of the creek's gorge. These crystals led a prospector to believe there would be ore there also. SHT passes through large birch forest, crosses powerline and private road and passes through red pine plantations.

▲ CRYSTAL CREEK CAMPSITE

TYPE: Regular
TENT PADS: 4
WATER: From Crystal Creek
SETTING: 1.5 miles west of Sugarloaf Rd.,
    on spur 200 yards off SHT
PREVIOUS CAMPSITE: 1.2 miles
NEXT CAMPSITE: 2.4 miles

3.5 (5.5)
SUGARLOAF RD.

After parking lot, SHT crosses Sugarloaf Road, crosses a stream on a bridge with spindle post railings, then travels through mixed forest and by an old beaver pond.

4.5 (4.5)
SUGARLOAF POND CAMPSITE

SHT continues through sometimes wet soil and passes several logging roads before Alfred's Pond.

▲ SUGARLOAF POND CAMPSITE

TYPE: Regular
TENT PADS: 4
WATER: pond
SETTING: 1.0 miles east of Sugarloaf Rd. on beaver pond
PREVIOUS CAMPSITE: 2.4 miles
NEXT CAMPSITE: 3.5 miles

5.8 (3.2)
ALFRED'S POND

Look for bog plants like the carnivorous pitcher plant and sundew, as well as sphagnum moss, orchids, and blue-flag iris. Floating walkway built in 1992 allows one to see everything without getting wet or damaging the bog. After pond, SHT travels through wet area, mostly on boardwalk. SHT climbs uphill, with possible view of Dyer's Lake through trees and, at 6.7 miles, of Lake Superior, then a steep downhill into birch valley.

7.9 (1.1)
DYER'S CREEK CAMPSITE
After crossing Dyer's Creek on a 25-foot bridge, look for spur on right side of SHT to campsite. SHT continues upstream along Two Island River, then ascends through mixed conifers.

▲ DYER'S CREEK CAMPSITE

TYPE: Regular
TENT PADS: 6
WATER: From Dyer's Creek
SETTING: 1.1 miles west of
  Co. Rd. 1
PREVIOUS CAMPSITE: 3.5 miles
NEXT CAMPSITE: 2.9 miles

8.6 (0.4)
1ST ROAD CROSSING
SHT comes to Dyer's Lake Rd., turns right and travels on road across active railroad tracks. SHT departs Dyer's Lake Rd. and goes back into woods on other side of tracks and crosses Cook Co. Rd. 1 (Cramer Rd.) to come to trailhead parking lot.

9.0 (0.0)
PARKING LOT OFF COOK CO. RD. 1
(CRAMER RD.)

BOGS ON THE TRAIL

Bogs are a type of wetland common in northern Minnesota, though less common along the Superior Hiking Trail. Bogs are characterized by a lush growth of sphagnum moss and high acidity. Since the bog is a nutrient-poor environment, some bog plants have evolved insect eating as a way of getting needed nutrients like nitrogen. The pitcher plant and sundew are two insectivorous plants common in the bogs in northern Minnesota.

The sundew is a tiny plant usually found on the edge of the mat close to water. It has sticky tipped hairs on its leaves that trap insects. The pitcher plant is much bigger, perhaps a foot across, and traps insects in its hollow, fluid-filled leaves. Bogs are fascinating places to explore, but please use the boardwalk provided.

WILDFLOWER CALENDAR FOR THE SUPERIOR HIKING TRAIL

MAY

Bloodroot	*Sanguinaria canadensis*
Violets	*Viola*
Wild Lily-of-the-Valley	*Maianthemum canadense*
Common Strawberry	*Fuagaria virginiana*
Marsh-marigold	*Caltha palustris*
Spring Beauty	*Claytonia virginica*
Wood Anemone	*Anemone quinquefolia*
Goldthread	*Coptis groenlandica*

JUNE

Nodding Trillium	*Trillium cernuum*
Starflower	*Trientalis borealis*
Bunchberry	*Cornus canadensis*
Columbine	*Aquilegia canadensis*
Moccasin Flower	*Cypripedium acaule*
Larger Blue-flag	*Iris versicolor*
Blue-bead Lily	*Clintonia borealis*

JULY

Meadowsweet	*Spiraea latifolia*
Spreading Dogbane	*Apocynum androsaemifolium*
Northern Bedstraw	*Galium boreale*
Indian-pipe	*Monotropa uniflora*
Heal-all	*Prunella vulgaris*
Cow-parsnip	*Heracleum maximum*

AUGUST

Goldenrods	*Solidago*
Large-leaf Aster	*Aster macrophyllus*
Fireweed	*Epilobium angustifolium*
Jewelweed	*Impatiens capensis*
Evening Primrose	*Oenothera*
Spotted Joe-Pye-Weed	*Eupatorium maculatum*

Cook County Road 1 to Temperance River State Park

START (END)
SHT parking lot on Cook Co. Rd. 1 (Cramer Rd.)

END (START)
Either Temperance River Wayside parking lot on Hwy. 61 or SHT parking lot on Forest Rd. 343

LENGTH OF TRAIL SECTION
8.0 miles

ACCESS AND PARKING
Nearest Hwy. 61 milepost: 78.9

Secondary road name and number: Cook Co. Rd. 1 (Cramer Rd.)

Go on Cook Co. Rd. 1 for 3.6 miles (first 1.7 miles paved, rest is gravel). Lot is on right 200 feet off Co. Rd. 1 and 0.1 miles before SHT crossing. Overnight okay.

ALTERNATE TRAILHEAD IN SCHROEDER
Nearest Hwy 61 milepost: 79.1 Turn north on Skou Road just past Cross River Falls. Go two blocks to little parking lot by sign. Overnight okay. Spur trail to main SHT is 1.5 miles. Trail starts by sharing ski trails, then eventually leaves ski trail and follows along Cross River high above river. Nice bench and view where spur meets main trail.

FACILITIES
At starting trailhead (farthest southwest): none

Designated campsites on this section of the SHT: five

SYNOPSIS
The climb to Tower Overlook through a rich old growth maple forest, the descent to Fredenberg Creek, and the hike along the marsh named Boney's Meadow, with a chance to see moose, set the stage for the highlight of the section, the historic Cross and Temperance Rivers.

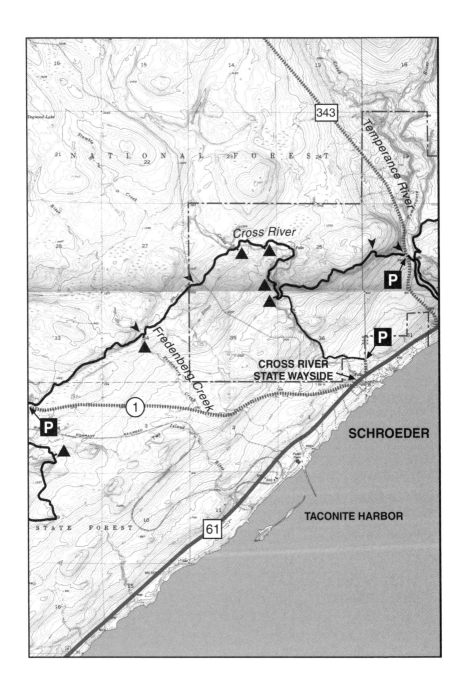

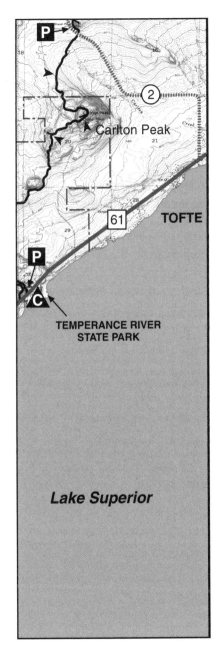

Carlton Peak

TOFTE

61

TEMPERANCE RIVER
STATE PARK

Lake Superior

MILE-BY-MILE DESCRIPTION

0.0 (8.0)
PARKING LOT
SHT passes through mixed conifer area, then ascends into the Superior National Forest Northern Hardwood Research Natural Area. This is one of the richest maple forests along the trail. The wildflower viewing along this section of trail in the spring is fantastic. SHT climbs to Tower Overlook, with a beautiful view of Lake Superior, then descends.

1.8 (6.2)
FREDENBERG CREEK
100 feet after footbridge, short spur trail to campsite. SHT follows creek, then follows edge of marsh, known locally as Boney's Meadow. This is a wonderful place to view waterfowl. Look for moose tracks near marsh.

▲ FREDENBERG CREEK CAMPSITE

TYPE: Regular
TENT PADS: 5
WATER: From Fredenberg Creek
SETTING: 1.8 miles east of Co. Rd. 1
PREVIOUS CAMPSITE: 2.9 miles
NEXT CAMPSITE: 2.0 miles

2.9 (5.1)
GASCO RD.
SHT crosses historic logging road, also a spur to the North

HISTORY OF THE CROSS RIVER

Hugging the banks of this spirited river for over a mile, the SHT gives ample opportunity to observe the various antics of the rushing water—site of any number of interesting historical events. The Voyageurs portaged this stretch of rapids to reach the calm headwaters, a chain of inland lakes, and eventually Lake Vermilion, near Tower. By the turn of the century, loggers had entered the watershed and used the river for the roaring spring log drive down to the boom at the mouth. This included putting a series of dams on the river. So "roaring" was the river that there are accounts of a bordello in what is now Schroeder. The logging business ceased operations in 1905 due in part to a smallpox epidemic.

Shore State Trail, a multipurpose trail linking Duluth and Grand Marais. SHT enters spruce plantation, then a hardwood forest, then descends to a lowland. SHT reaches the bluff of the Cross River.

3.8 (4.2)
FALLS ON CROSS RIVER

Great view of falls, excellent lunch or rest stop. The river is highlight of this section. SHT follows edge of river up and down steep bluffs. Look for beaver activity on sidestreams.

▲ FALLS CAMPSITE

TYPE: Regular
TENT PADS: 3
WATER: From Cross River
SETTING: Uphill from Cross River
PREVIOUS CAMPSITE: 2.0 miles
NEXT CAMPSITE: 0.8 miles

▲ LEDGE CAMPSITE

TYPE: Regular
TENT PADS: 2
WATER: From Cross River
SETTING: Uphill from Cross River
PREVIOUS CAMPSITE: 0.8 miles
NEXT CAMPSITE: 0.8 miles

5.3 (2.7)
CROSS RIVER CAMPSITES AND BRIDGE

SHT crosses bridge over river. At the trail junction after bridge, SHT goes upstream, spur trail 1.5 miles to Skou Rd. in Schroeder goes downstream. Main SHT follows bluff, then travels along ridgeline, with views of Lake Superior and Taconite Harbor operations.

Note the absence of red or white pines, evidence of the pine logging operations early this century. SHT passes through red pine plantation.

▲ NORTH CROSS RIVER CAMPSITE

TYPE: Regular
TENT PADS: 2
WATER: From Cross River
SETTING: On Cross River
PREVIOUS CAMPSITE: 0.8 miles
NEXT CAMPSITE: 0.1 miles

▲ SOUTH CROSS RIVER CAMPSITE

TYPE: Regular
TENT PADS: 4
WATER: From Cross River
SETTING: 1.7 miles up spur trail from Schroeder, above river
PREVIOUS CAMPSITE: 0.1 miles
NEXT CAMPSITE: 9.1 miles (or use Temperance River State Park)

6.4 (1.6)
TOP OF RIDGE

SHT continues with long and sometimes steep descents through birch/aspen forest.

7.2 (0.8)
TEMPERANCE RIVER RD. (FOREST RD. 343)

SHT reaches road at parking lot 0.9 miles up Forest Rd. 343 from Hwy. 61. Either end hike here or cross road and continue along Temperance River to wayside parking lot. SHT heads downstream as the Temperance changes from a wide, quiet river to a roaring cascade in narrow gorges. SHT eventually joins state park XC trail for about 0.3 miles, then turns sharply left to follow edge of second gorge for about 200 yards before reaching the snowmobile bridge across the Temperance cascades. After crossing bridge, spur trail goes downstream 0.2 miles to parking lot. Main SHT goes upstream to Carlton Peak and beyond.

8.0 (0.0)
TEMPERANCE RIVER WAYSIDE PARKING LOT
On Hwy. 61.

Temperance River State Park to Britton Peak

START (END)
Temperance River Wayside parking lot on Hwy. 61

END (START)
Britton Peak parking lot on Cook Co. Rd. 2 (Sawbill Trail)

LENGTH OF TRAIL SECTION
4.8 miles

SAFETY CONCERNS
• Cliffs on Carlton Peak

ACCESS AND PARKING
Nearest Hwy. 61 milepost: 80.3 Secondary road name and number: none

Trailhead is on north side of Hwy. 61, on east side of the river. Look for SHT sign

No overnight parking in wayside parking lot. Can park overnight at lot in state park (permit required).

FACILITIES
Bathrooms, outhouses, telephone, drinking water, campground

Designated campsites on this section of the SHT: none

SYNOPSIS
This is one of the most easily accessible sections of the SHT and one of the most hiked. The hike to Carlton Peak from either direction climbs steeply, and the short but steep scramble to the top of the peak has ample rewards of incredible views. Coming from Temperance River State Park, the hiker also gets to see the amazing Temperance River, roaring deep in a dark basaltic canyon.

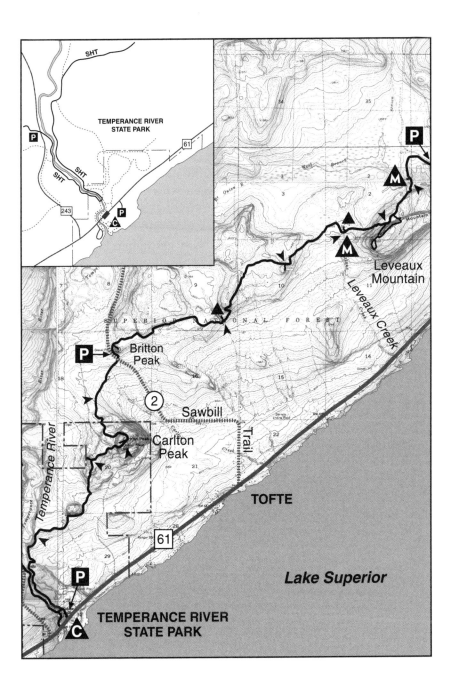

Lake Superior

TOFTE

Leveaux
Mountain

Leveaux Creek

Britton
Peak

Sawbill

Carlton
Peak

Trail

Temperance River

TEMPERANCE RIVER
STATE PARK

TEMPERANCE RIVER
STATE PARK

TEMPERANCE RIVER
STATE PARK

The Temperance River was presumably so named because, unlike other North Shore streams, this river had no bar at its mouth. The 500 acre park is best known for its deep, narrow river gorge, waterfalls, and the glacial potholes that dot the river valley. Fishing is popular on the Temperance and nearby Cross Rivers, where several species of trout and salmon have been stocked and have become established. Two campgrounds with a total of 50 sites are popular because of their lakeside location. Eight miles of trails connect with the North Shore State Trail, the SHT and Superior National Forest trails, and provide recreational use year around. Picnic sites are located along Lake Superior adjacent to the lower campground.

0.0 (4.8)
TRAILHEAD AT TEMPERANCE RIVER WAYSIDE PARKING LOT

This spur trail joins the main SHT at the bridge 0.2 miles up the gorge from the trailhead—look for interpretive signs. Trails fork and wander a lot, but SHT continues upstream. SHT joins XC trail at a switchback and climbs high on rim over river.

1.2 (3.6)
SHT LEAVES RIVER

SHT enters scrubby woods, then an aspen forest. SHT shares the Lynx XC ski trail. Look for signs of old white pines and fire. Two major fires have swept through here. Look for national forest survey lines, the wide straight cuts through the forest. SHT turns steeply uphill, leaving XC trail and climbing through birches.

2.6 (2.2)
OVERLOOK SPUR

Look for sign and follow spur 80 yards for a view of Lake Superior, Temperance River valley, and Taconite Harbor. Main SHT continues through a pure birch forest, past a spur with an old access road and ski trail to Carlton Peak. SHT begins gradual ascent counterclockwise around Carlton Peak, through large fallen boulders. This is a popular rock climbing site and the only difficult hiking on this section.

3.1 (1.7)
SPUR TRAIL TO SUMMIT

Well worth the trip to the top. Trail register at the spur trail junction leading to summit on left. After leaving summit, a spur trail to "Ted Tofte Overlook" is on right. Main SHT continues along high rock walls. Watch for view of Britton Peak and Raven's Ridge above Tofte.

4.0 (0.8)
LYNX XC SKI TRAIL

SHT travels through maple forest, then a spruce plantation. Lots of wooden walkways to cross muddy areas. SHT reenters woods, crosses ski trail, then crosses Sawbill Trail and winds into the Britton Peak parking lot.

4.8 (0.0)
BRITTON PEAK PARKING LOT

CARLTON PEAK

The high points on the North Shore landscape exist because they are made of rocks that have been more resistant to weathering and erosion over the billion years since they were formed. Carlton Peak is a prime example, made of several huge blocks of whitish anorthosite rock. These blocks were carried or floated up from the base of the earth's crust, 25 or 30 miles below, suspended in molten diabase magma. With very few natural fractures, these anorthosite blocks or "inclusions" also make up many of the knobs and hills in and around Silver Bay and Tettegouche State Park.

A climb to the top of Carlton Peak reveals some tremendous views, which is why this was the site of a fire tower up until the 1950s (the foundation is all that is left of the tower).

Britton Peak to Oberg Mountain

START (END)
Britton Peak access on Cook Co. Rd. 2 (Sawbill Trail)

END (START)
Oberg Mountain parking lot on Forest Rd. 336 (Onion River Rd.)

LENGTH OF TRAIL SECTION
5.7 miles

ACCESS AND PARKING
Nearest Hwy. 61 milepost: 82.8

Secondary road name and number: Cook Co. Rd. 2 (Sawbill Trail)

Go 2.7 miles north on Sawbill Trail. Parking area on right. Overnight okay.

FACILITIES
At starting trailhead (farthest southwest): outhouse

Designated campsites on this section of the SHT: four

SYNOPSIS
This section crosses the Sugarbush cross-country ski trail system several times. The section, one of the easier of the SHT, begins as an easy, rolling path through maple and birch forest, with a carpet of leaves underfoot in autumn. The topography becomes more dramatic in the central section and the maple and birch give way to spruce, balsam, and cedar around the beaver pond. From the pond the SHT ascends to the Leveaux Mountain loop and on to the parking area. Wet and seasonally wet ground is typical along this section.

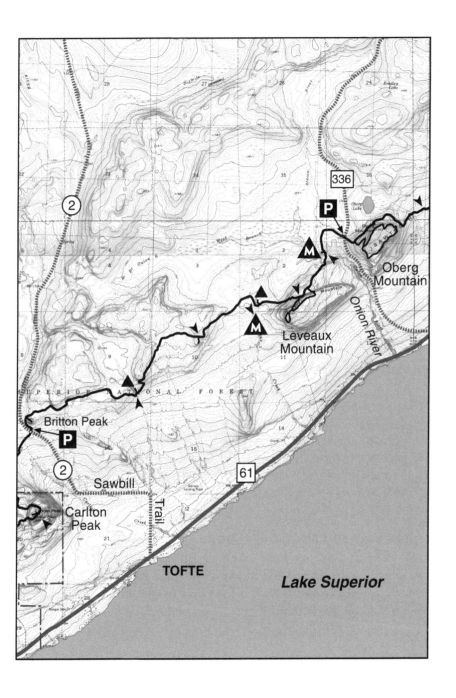

MILE-BY-MILE DESCRIPTION

0.0 (5.7)
PARKING AREA
Right after SHT leaves trailhead, spur leads steeply up 300 yards to overlook near top of Britton Peak. The view from the top is dominated by Carlton Peak in the distance. There is a memorial for W.L. Britton, a WWII veteran who worked for the Forest Service for two years. His ashes were strewn on Britton Peak in 1947. Main SHT continues through dense sugar maple forest. SHT crosses ski trails frequently, at 0.2, 1.2, and 1.4 miles. Ski trails have blue blazes. SHT also crosses numerous planks and corduroy in wet spots.

1.6 (4.1)
WOODEN BRIDGE AT SPRINGDALE CREEK
SHT campsite just east of bridge. SHT crosses XC trail, then climbs through young sugar maple stand to an overlook with a view of Lake Superior and Apostle Islands 30 miles away. SHT crosses old roadbed.

▲ SPRINGDALE CREEK CAMPSITE

TYPE: Regular
TENT PADS: 4
WATER: From creek—unreliable during dry conditions
SETTING: 1.6 miles from Sawbill Trail
PREVIOUS CAMPSITE: 9.1 miles
   (or use Temperance River State Park)
NEXT CAMPSITE: 2.5 miles

2.9 (2.8)
SPUR TRAIL TO CEDAR OVERLOOK
Steep 200-yard climb to view of Lake Superior and Sawtooth Mountains, including Leveaux, Oberg, and Moose Mountains. SHT continues along ridge, then crosses ski trail. Forest begins to change to spruce and balsam. Lots of diamonds marking XC trails throughout this area.

4.2 (1.5)
BRIDGE ACROSS LEVEAUX BEAVER POND
Look for the beaver lodge to the north, and watch for moose. SHT campsite 0.2 miles past bridge. SHT crosses XC trail, enters cedar grove,

then enters maple forest beneath the cliffs of Leveaux Mountain.

⛺ WEST LEVEAUX POND CAMPSITE

TYPE: Multi-group
TENT PADS: 8
WATER: From beaver pond
SETTING: 1.3 miles to Forest Rd. 336
PREVIOUS CAMPSITE: 2.5 miles
NEXT CAMPSITE: 0.1 miles

▲ EAST LEVEAUX POND CAMPSITE

TYPE: Regular
TENT PADS: 4
WATER: From beaver pond
SETTING: 1.2 miles to Forest Rd. 336. Nice view of beaver pond.
PREVIOUS CAMPSITE: 0.1 miles
NEXT CAMPSITE: 1.2 miles

TRAIL MAINTENANCE VOLUNTEERS

Is the trail too muddy for your tastes? Are more boardwalks needed? Is there a newly fallen tree that needs to be cut? The Superior Hiking Trail is maintained by us, the trail users. If you or your group would like to lend a helping hand, let us know. Contact the SHTA to volunteer.

4.5 (1.2)
WEST JUNCTION OF LEVEAUX MTN. SPUR TRAIL

Spur trail goes to top of Leveaux Mountain for several grand Lake Superior overlooks. The west end of spur trail is less steep than the east end. Leveaux Mountain spur trail rejoins SHT at 4.7 (1.0).

5.1 (0.6)
BRIDGE AT ONION RIVER

Campsite is in spruce forest 0.1 miles past river.

⛺ ONION RIVER CAMPSITE

TYPE: Multi-group
TENT PADS: 8
WATER: From Onion River
SETTING: 0.5 miles from Forest Rd. 336, high above Onion River
PREVIOUS CAMPSITE: 1.2 miles
NEXT CAMPSITE: 2.0 miles

5.7 (0.0)
OBERG MOUNTAIN TRAILHEAD PARKING LOT

Oberg Mountain to Lutsen

START (END)
Oberg Mountain parking lot on Forest Rd. 336 (Onion River Rd.)

END (START)
Lutsen Ski Area, on Cook Co. Rd. 5 (Ski Hill Rd.)

LENGTH OF TRAIL SECTION
7.0 miles

SAFETY CONCERNS
• Steep overlooks on Oberg Mountain

• Steep slopes on both sides of Moose Mountain

ACCESS AND PARKING
Nearest Hwy. 61 milepost: 87.5

Secondary road name and number: Forest Rd. 336 (Onion River Rd.)

Turnoff onto Onion River Rd. is marked by SHT sign and XC ski sign, but is easy to miss otherwise. Go north on Forest Rd. 336 approximately 2.2 miles to parking area on left side of road, opposite of Oberg trailhead. Overnight okay.

FACILITIES
At starting trailhead (farthest southwest): outhouse

Designated campsites on this section of the SHT: three

SYNOPSIS
This section has a bit of everything, from the scenic overlooks of Oberg Mountain and Moose Mountain to the dense maple forests of the northeastern end. After the optional spur loop to Oberg Mountain, the main SHT winds through boreal forests of birch, spruce, balsam fir, and alder, then climbs to the top of Moose Mountain, where the views in all directions are rewarding. The ups and downs make this a challenging section. The last three miles go through a rich maple forest before emerging at the gorge of the Poplar River. This section was constructed by the Forest Service and is one of the oldest sections of the SHT.

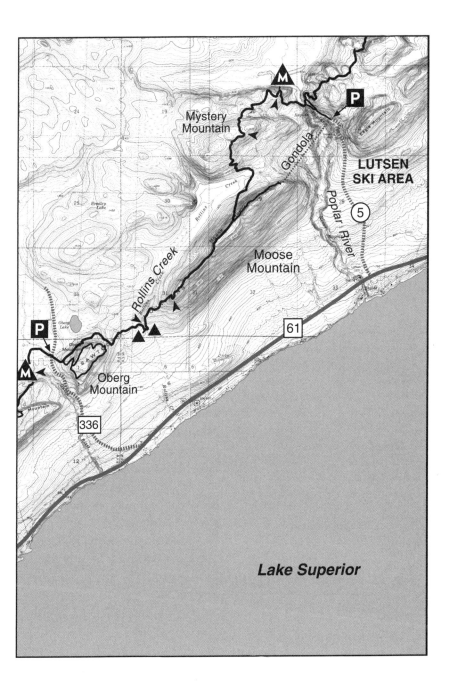

OBERG LOOP

This is a 1.8-mile loop around the summit of Oberg Mountain. Oberg is covered by a rich maple forest, which gives out only at the many scenic overlooks. Work your way counterclockwise around the summit for about eight different overlooks in all directions, starting with Leveaux Mountain and Lake Superior (and a distant Carlton Peak), then Moose Mountain, and finally inland to Oberg Lake and the rolling crests of inland ridges. Trail is well-maintained and overlooks are developed for safety. One of the overlooks has a picnic table. This is a great hike any time of year, but especially in the fall when the colors of this mountain and Leveaux Mountain are at their peak.

MILE-BY-MILE DESCRIPTION

0.0 (7.0)
OBERG MOUNTAIN PARKING LOT

SHT leaves from east side of parking lot, up some wooden steps. Junction of Oberg Mountain loop at 0.2 miles, a great side trip of about 1.8 miles (see sidebar). Main SHT continues northeast around the base of Oberg Mountain through dense shrubs. Oberg Lake visible through trees to the north. SHT descends into wet area, then crosses a creek.

1.2 (5.8)
JUNCTION WITH XC TRAIL

SHT goes straight across XC trail and also snowmobile trail. Mixed forest, with tall aspen, a huge cedar tree, and lots of bluebead lily. At one point in this stretch you can see Oberg Mountain and pick out the shape of a human face high in the rock wall. Just before Rollins Creek is a short spur to campsite.

▲ **WEST ROLLINS CREEK CAMPSITE**

TYPE: Regular
TENT PADS: 5
WATER: From Rollins Creek
SETTING: 1.6 miles east of Forest Rd. 336, in a large cedar grove
PREVIOUS CAMPSITE: 2.0 miles
NEXT CAMPSITE: 0.1 miles

1.6 (5.4)
PLANK BRIDGE OVER ROLLINS CREEK

SHT follows creek upstream a ways, then ascends from valley up flank of Moose Mountain, through yellow birch, cedar, and spruce, then paper birch, aspen, and fir. SHT gets steeper and steeper. Look for northern plants like shinleaf pyrola and twinflower near switchbacks on south side of Moose Mountain.

▲ **EAST ROLLINS CREEK CAMPSITE**

TYPE: Regular
TENT PADS: 3
WATER: From Rollins Creek
SETTING: 1.7 miles east of Forest Rd. 336
PREVIOUS CAMPSITE: 0.1 mile
NEXT CAMPSITE: 4.5 miles

2.2 (4.8)
SOUTHWEST END OF MOOSE MOUNTAIN RIDGETOP

Short, unmaintained spur to partial overlook of Lake Superior and Oberg Mountain. Moose Mountain is 1,688 feet above sea level and 1,086 feet above lake. SHT winds along ridgetop, with occasional views on both sides. Forest here is quite northern in composition, with spruce, birch, and balsam fir, and little undergrowth. Listen for the chatter of red squirrels.

3.4 (3.6)
SPUR TO TO GONDOLA

This 0.8 mile spur goes along the north side of Moose Mountain to the top of the gondola. A fun day hike is to take the gondola to the top of Moose Mountain and then hike back to the chalet, a total of 3.5 miles. SHT descends along north side of Moose Mountain. Descent is steep and rugged, with large basaltic outcroppings and a dark, shaded forest. SHT continues north, across plank bridge (headwaters of Rollins Creek, which SHT also crosses 1.5 miles to the SW), and enters maple forest. Note all ages of maple trees, from seedling to mature. SHT ascends after climbing out of creek valley.

5.2 (1.8)
OVERLOOK
Small, unmarked overlook of Lutsen ski hills, gondola, and down Poplar River valley to Lake Superior. SHT continues in maple forest, then forest changes to birch and spruce. 400 yards before campsite, there is a spur to overlook marked by sign with views of Poplar River valley.

6.1 (0.9)
CAMPSITE
Campsite is just off SHT. Just past campsite is 10-yard spur to overlook over Poplar River, spruce swamp. SHT descends into wet area with scrubby alders, birches, thimbleberries, and raspberries. SHT turns left onto Lutsen XC ski and bike trail (junction marked by SHT sign). SHT follows Poplar River gorge downstream on wide trailbed, then crosses river on a wide bridge over a spectacular waterfall. 0.4- mile spur to parking lot goes downstream. Follow spur 0.1 miles to junction with dirt road, then another 0.3 miles to parking lot at Lutsen Ski hill. Watch signs carefully. Main SHT continues on toward Caribou Trail (Co. Rd. 4).

▲ MYSTERY MOUNTAIN CAMPSITE

TYPE: Multi-group
TENT PADS: 6
WATER: 0.5 miles away at Poplar River
SETTING: 1.0 miles to Co. Rd. 5, overlooking Poplar River Valley
PREVIOUS CAMPSITE: 4.5 miles
NEXT CAMPSITE: 2.1 miles

7.0 (0.0)
LUTSEN SKI AREA TRAILHEAD PARKING LOT
Parking lot is adjacent to Papa Charlie's Restaurant.

Lutsen to Caribou Trail

START (END)
Lutsen ski area, on Cook Co. Rd. 5 (Ski Hill Rd.)

END (START)
Cook Co. Rd. 4 (Caribou Trail)

LENGTH OF TRAIL SECTION
6.4 miles

ACCESS AND PARKING
Nearest Hwy. 61 milepost: 90.1

Secondary road name and number: Cook Co. Rd. 5 (Ski Hill Rd.)

Go 2.9 miles to end of road, past Alpine Slide, gondola terminal, and Papa Charlie's Restaurant. Parking for 8–10 cars. Overnight okay.

FACILITIES
At starting trailhead (farthest southwest): bathrooms, telephone, drinking water, restaurant, gift shop, lodging

Designated campsites on this section of the SHT: four

SYNOPSIS
This is a very scenic segment of the SHT, with a diverse forest ranging from a mature maple canopy through mixed birch/aspen/pine and spruce. Stretches parallel the winding Poplar River and breathtaking Lake Agnes, and there are several open vistas of the Poplar River valley. In late summer it is a mushroom-hunter's heaven in terms of variety and supply.

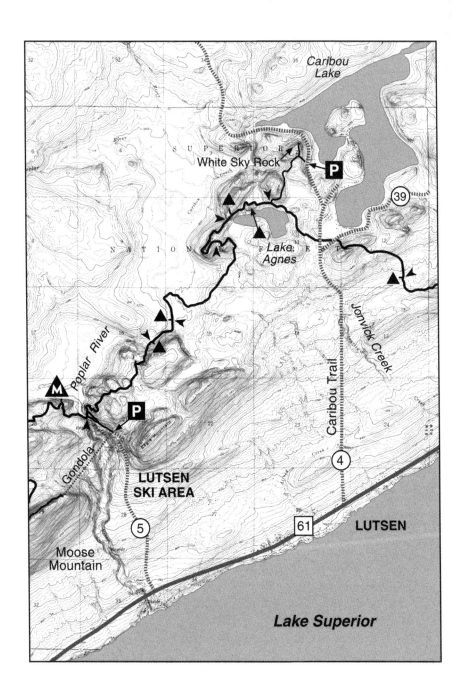

MILE-BY-MILE DESCRIPTION

0.0 (6.4)
TRAILHEAD PARKING LOT

Follow 0.4-mile spur trail through mixed forest. Spur forks off old road to left after 0.3 miles and comes to main SHT after 0.1 miles. SHT winds northeast through switchbacks to overlook on ski area. SHT then enters mature maple forest and gently rolling terrain. The SHT crosses a ski/bike trail, then continues to Glove Overlook, a rock outcrop with views north and west of Poplar River valley. SHT winds down through pine and aspen forest.

1.5 (4.9)
POPLAR RIVER WEST CAMPSITE

SHT follows river after campsite, crosses a snowmobile trail at 2.0 miles, which has a bridge over the river. This area is heavily travelled by moose, so keep an eye out for tracks, antler rubs, and the huge brown animal.

▲ **WEST POPLAR RIVER CAMPSITE**

TYPE: Regular
TENT PADS: 3
WATER: From Poplar River
SETTING: 1.5 miles east of Lutsen, on the river
PREVIOUS CAMPSITE: 2.1 miles
NEXT CAMPSITE: 0.6 miles

ECOLOGY OF NORTH AND SOUTH SLOPES

Many factors lead to the particular kind of trees and other plants at any given point along the trail. One factor that is often apparent along the trail is the difference between north- and south-facing slopes. Experienced hikers know the old wisdom that moss grows on the north side of trees. The same holds true for the ridgelines of the North Shore. Along the ridgeline, the forest on the southern or Lake side receives significantly more sunshine than the forest on the northern, inland side. This added sunshine makes the forest warmer and drier, an environment friendly to trees of the northern hardwood type, such as birch, aspen, oak, and maple. The cooler, moister north-facing slopes have, in general, a more boreal feel, with spruces and fir, as well as the proverbial moss. Keep an eye out for these subtle changes!

2.1 (4.3)
POPLAR RIVER EAST CAMPSITE
Lots of moose sign. SHT goes through spruce swamp with many log footbridges. SHT leaves low area and ascends into mature maple forest.

▲ **EAST POPLAR RIVER CAMPSITE**

TYPE: Regular
TENT PADS: 2
WATER: From Poplar River
SETTING: 2.1 miles east of Lutsen, on the river
PREVIOUS CAMPSITE: 0.6 miles
NEXT CAMPSITE: 3.0 miles

4.0 (2.4)
OVERLOOK ON POPLAR RIVER
First of three outstanding overlooks of Poplar River valley. All three are good break spots, with views of valley and river snaking far below, also of Lake Superior.

5.0 (1.4)
AGNES CREEK BRIDGE
SHT climbs steeply to dramatic Lake Agnes overlook by trail register. SHT descends to lakeshore and steep spur to campsite high above lake. After the campsites, the trail continues along the north side of Lake Agnes to the spur trail junction.

▲ **WEST LAKE AGNES CAMPSITE**

TYPE: Regular
TENT PADS: 4
WATER: From Lake Agnes
SETTING: 1.3 miles west of Caribou Trail,
    in maple grove overlooking Lake Agnes
PREVIOUS CAMPSITE: 3.0 miles
NEXT CAMPSITE: 0.3 miles

▲ EAST LAKE AGNES CAMPSITE

TYPE: Regular
TENT PADS: 4
WATER: From Lake Agnes
SETTING: 1.0 miles to
    Caribou Trail, right on lake
PREVIOUS CAMPSITE: 0.3 miles
NEXT CAMPSITE: 2.4 miles

5.6 (0.8)
SPUR TRAIL TO PARKING LOT

Sign clearly marks directions and mileage. The main SHT continues along Lake Agnes and then continues through mixed forest to Caribou Trail 1.0 miles south of parking lot.

The spur trail turns north from Lake Agnes 0.8 miles to Caribou Trail parking lot. It passes Cedar Hill, goes through a narrow rock canyon where a staircase has been sculpted from a single log, crosses a snowmobile trail, and heads up to White Sky Rock, overlooking Caribou Lake. Trail descends from there to parking lot. Turns on spur trail are marked by arrows.

6.4 (0.0)
CARIBOU TRAIL TRAILHEAD PARKING LOT

LUTSEN-TOFTE TOURISM ASSOCIATION

Imagine having the task of promoting and marketing tourism in an area that is rich with rugged, beautiful landscapes featuring the largest freshwater lake in the world. Throw in recreational opportunities for all seasons. That is the job of the Lutsen-Tofte Tourism Association (LTTA). This organization includes most of the lodging accommodations from Little Marais to just east of the Cascade River. The participating businesses in this area offer a wide variety of accommodations from rustic to luxurious, and dining options range from a shore lunch picnic to white linen table cloths. The LTTA also offers lodge-to-lodge hiking packages along the SHT, allowing hikers to enjoy the best of both worlds: wilderness hiking as a backpacker would experience during the day, followed by fine lodging and meals during the night. Many resorts also offer shuttle service to trailheads and route information for their guests.

Caribou Trail to Cascade River State Park

START (END)
Cook Co. Rd. 4 (Caribou Trail)

END (START)
Cascade River State Park, on
Hwy. 61

LENGTH OF TRAIL SECTION
11.0 miles

ACCESS AND PARKING
Nearest Hwy. 61 milepost: 92

Secondary road name and number: Cook Co. Rd. 4 (Caribou Trail). Parking lot is 4.1 miles up Caribou Trail (SHT crosses at 3.1 miles). Room for 5-6 cars. There is also a public boat landing for Caribou Lake with additional parking. There are two ways to access the main SHT.

SPUR TRAIL
From parking area cross Caribou Trail and follow spur trail 0.8 miles back toward White Sky Rock and Lake Agnes to main trail.

ROAD WALK
Walk 1 mile down Caribou Trail to place where main SHT crosses.

FACILITIES
At starting trailhead (farthest southwest): outhouse at Caribou Lake boat landing

Designated campsites on this section of the SHT: three

SYNOPSIS
This section follows along ridgelines with many views of Lake Superior and inland ridges of Sawtooth range. The variety of habitats is as broad as anywhere on the SHT, with everything from mature maple forests to dense groves of cedar, from a massive beaver pond to wide-open hillsides. It begins with a moderately steep ascent but drops gently to a valley and crosses a beaver dam. It crosses several scenic creeks and travels through Cascade River State Park.

MILE-BY-MILE DESCRIPTION

0.0 (11.0)
CARIBOU TRAIL PARKING LOT
From the parking lot, take the spur trail 0.8 miles to reach the main
SHT. Cross Caribou Trail (Co. Rd. 4) and go west and then south to
reach main trail by Lake Agnes. There is an optional 0.15 mile spur
trail to White Sky Rock off the spur trail with overlook of Caribou
Lake. At main SHT, go east 0.8 miles through maple forest and cross
Caribou Trail once more.

1.6 (9.4)
CARIBOU TRAIL
SHT crosses ditch, passes some corduroy boardwalk and wet spots,
and the climbing wall of the Cathedral of the Pines camp. Trail
crosses Co. Rd. 39. This land all belongs to the camp, so please stay
on trail. Steep climb through big cedar and maple to ridge with vista
of Caribou Lake. Many trails which are part of the camp cross SHT.
SHT travels through maple forest. Maples turn to alder thicket as
SHT approaches Jonvick Creek and crosses some small plank bridges.
Watch for woodcock near pond.

▲ JONVICK CREEK CAMPSITE

TYPE: Regular
TENT PADS: 2
WATER: From beaver pond
SETTING: 1.4 miles east of Caribou Trail, on beaver pond
PREVIOUS CAMPSITE: 2.4 miles
NEXT CAMPSITE: 2.2 miles

3.0 (8.0)
JONVICK CREEK CROSSING
Cross boardwalk built on top of beaver dam. Immediately after dam,
SHT crosses a wide, grassy snowmobile trail, then meanders through
mixed forest. SHT crosses XC ski trail from Solbakken Resort, then
ascends gentle slope through mature aspen to maple grove and views
of Lake Superior on top of ridge. SHT goes through spruce plantation with wide views of Lake Superior, crosses two dirt roads (one
called the Hall Rd.), then reenters maples. SHT continues along

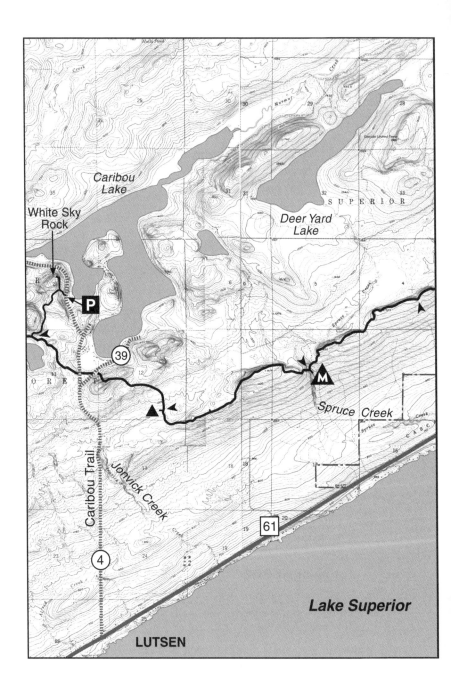

Caribou
Lake

White Sky
Rock

P

39

Caribou Trail

Jonvick Creek

4

Deer Yard
Lake

S U P E R I O R

M

Spruce Creek

61

Lake Superior

LUTSEN

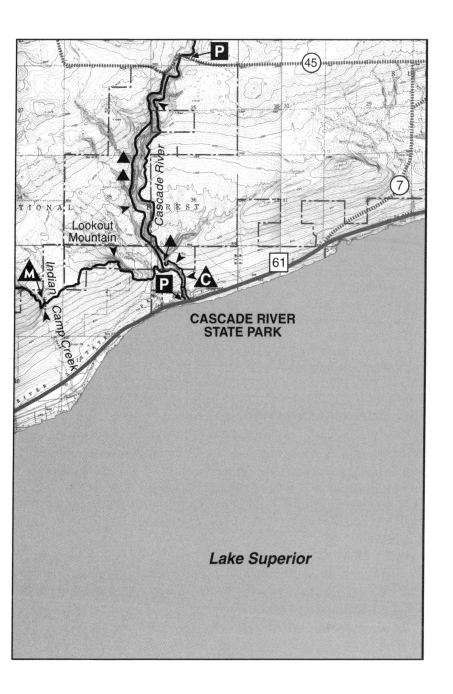

CASCADE RIVER
STATE PARK

Lake Superior

ridgeline in cedar, birch, and pine, with views of inland ridges, then descends sharply to Spruce Creek. As with other ridges on the SHT, hawks are visible from this ridge during fall migration.

5.2 (5.8)
SPRUCE CREEK CROSSING

Campsite on east side of bridge. SHT ascends to ridgeline of birch, spruce, fir, cedar, and pine. SHT crosses a snowmobile trail to another ridgeline with views of Lake Superior and inland ridges, then slopes down to an open, sometimes muddy area and back up to another ridgeline with almost pure maple.

▲ SPRUCE CREEK CAMPSITE

TYPE: Multi-group
TENT PADS: 7
WATER: From Spruce Creek
SETTING: 3.6 miles east of
  Caribou Trail
PREVIOUS CAMPSITE: 2.2 miles
NEXT CAMPSITE: 3.3 miles

6.8 (4.2)
JUNCTION WITH SNOWMOBILE TRAIL

SHT uses wider snowmobile trail for 0.5 miles, continuing up and down along grassy, open ridge. Watch carefully as SHT leaves snowmobile trail sharply to left, then climbs ridge to view of inland ridges and the lakeshore toward Grand Marais, before steeply descending along curving ridgeline and cliff edge, past 10-yard spur to viewpoint.

8.5 (2.5)
INDIAN CAMP CREEK

Campsite on east side of creek. SHT crosses a snowmobile trail, meanders through woods of cedar, birch, and aspen, then down to wooden walkways across potentially muddy area. Downed and dying fir are victims of spruce budworm infestation. SHT then climbs through aspen woods, meets state park XC trail and follows this trail past a state park trail map to junction with state park fee campsites. SHT continues up to Lookout Mountain overlook.

⚠️ INDIAN CAMP CREEK CAMPSITE

TYPE: Multi-group
TENT PADS: 6
WATER: From Indian Camp Creek
SETTING: 2.5 miles west of
   Cascade River State Park
PREVIOUS CAMPSITE: 3.3 miles
NEXT CAMPSITE: 3.3 miles if fol-
   lowing west side of Cascade
   River; 3.2 miles if following east
   side of Cascade River (or use
   Cascade River State Park)

9.7 (1.3)
LOOKOUT MOUNTAIN

Benches and a trail register at overlook. SHT descends, crossing XC trail to Cascade Lodge. SHT passes large stumps left over from white pine logging, then crosses another XC trail. SHT crosses a small stream, and then joins Cascade River State Park trail. SHT turns (left) onto XC trail soon after crossing stream. Watch for signed trail junction at top of the famous "96 Steps." Main trail continues upstream from this junction. The spur trail to Hwy. 61 parking lot follows dramatic series of falls. Bridge on spur trail provides access to SHT on east side of river.

10.8 (0.2)
CASCADE RIVER BRIDGE

Spur trails to the Hwy. 61 parking lot go down both sides of the river.

11.0 (0.0)
CASCADE RIVER WAYSIDE PARKING LOT

CASCADE RIVER STATE PARK

Named for the series of stair-stepping waterfalls on the Cascade River, Cascade River State Park offers numerous spectacular views along trails and bridges that follow and cross the river. Its 2,865 acres follow a half-mile-wide band along 1.5 miles of Lake Superior shoreline. Cascade served as an Emergency Conservation Work (ECW) camp during the 1930s. Their handiwork includes the trails that follow the river. Within the park are eighteen miles of hiking trails, many of which connect with the Superior Hiking Trail and other trails in the Superior National Forest. Located within the park is an enclosed picnic shelter, a modern campground with 40 drive-in sites, two group camp sites, and five backpack sites, one located on the Lake Superior shore. A small picnic area is also located along Lake Superior.

Cascade River State Park to Bally Creek Road

START (END)
Cascade River Wayside on Hwy. 61

END (START)
Forest Rd. 158 (Bally Creek Rd.)

LENGTH OF TRAIL SECTION
9.6 miles using east side of river; 9.7 miles using west side of river

SAFETY CONCERNS
• Several steeper slopes can be slippery when wet, particularly on descents

• Lots of roots and rocks on parts of trail

ACCESS AND PARKING
HWY. 61 TRAILHEAD
Nearest Hwy. 61 milepost: 99.9

Secondary road name and number: none

Two parking options:

1) Park on north side of Hwy. 61, day use only
2) For overnight parking, use the lot in the campground at state park. There is a second trailhead here. State Park permit required.

ACCESS AND PARKING:
COOK CO. RD. 45 TRAILHEAD
Nearest Hwy. 61 milepost: 101.5

Secondary road name and number: go 2.0 miles on Co. Rd. 7 until junction with Co. Rd. 44, north (straight) on Co. Rd. 44 for 0.5 miles, west (left) on Co. Rd. 45 for 2.6 miles.

Park on right just before bridge. Lot holds 12 cars. Overnight okay.

FACILITIES
At starting trailhead: bathrooms, outhouses, telephone, drinking water (all in state park facilities)

Designated campsites on this section of the SHT: five

SYNOPSIS
After ascending the scenic Cascade River valley, this section of the SHT enters a remote area. The Hidden Falls section is a highlight, as well as the remote woods and tree plantations east of Co. Rd. 45.

The 7.8-mile Cascade River loop is a popular daytrip, up one side of the river and down the other.

MILE-BY-MILE DESCRIPTION

0.0 (9.5)
TRAILHEAD
Directly east of the Hwy. 61 bridge over the Cascade River, behind the guard rail. This is a spur trail and there is no SHT marker. Spur trail climbs up steps. Look for Cascade Falls below.

0.2 (9.3)
FOOTBRIDGE AT FALLS JUNCTION
At this point SHT goes up either the west or east banks of the Cascade River. This is a popular 7.8-mile loop hike up one side and down the other.

FOLLOWING WEST SIDE OF CASCADE RIVER
From bridge over falls trail climbs to the "96 Steps," an ambitious bit of engineering that brings the SHT down to the riverside above the cascades. Like most North Shore streams, this rather gentle river becomes the famed cascades only as it passes through bedrock downstream.

1.4 (8.1)
SPUR TRAIL TO "SECRET WATERFALL"
Spur runs 0.3 miles to the "secret waterfall." 0.2 miles past spur, SHT passes an old mine site. There is an old shaft on the right side of trail which is now full of water, and the remains of some building foundations on the trailside. SHT then crosses bridge over tributary of the Cascade River. Large cedars dominate on this stretch of trail and the treadway is rocky and full of roots.

▲ **BIG WHITE PINE CAMPSITE**

TYPE: Regular
TENT PADS: 3
WATER: From small creek
SETTING: 1.6 miles from Cascade River Wayside
PREVIOUS CAMPSITE: 3.3 miles (or use State Park)
NEXT CAMPSITE: 0.5 miles

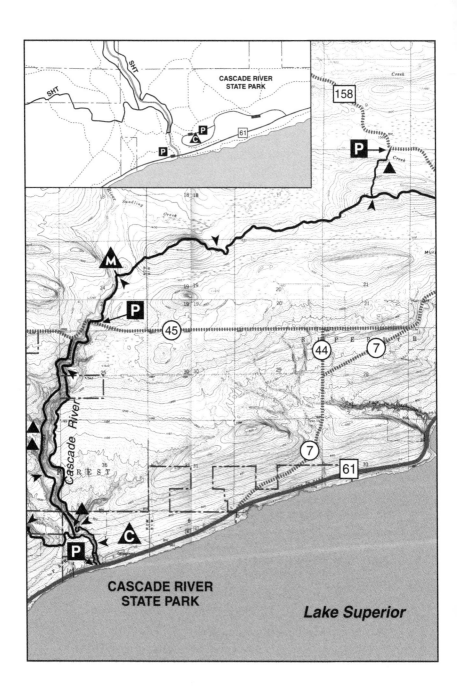

Lake Superior

CASCADE RIVER STATE PARK

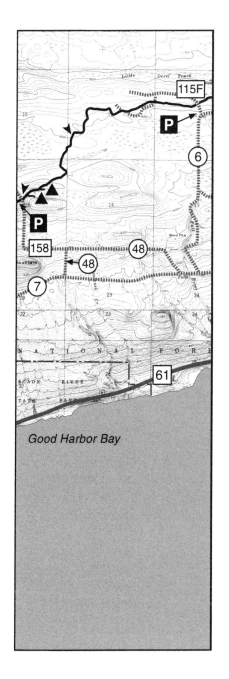

Good Harbor Bay

GEOLOGY OF NORTH SHORE WATERFALLS

The North Shore is blessed by many beautiful waterfalls, including several that give the name to the Cascade River. The abundance of waterfalls is basically the result of two factors: 1) the profound erosion of the Lake Superior basin by the great Ice Age glaciers, which led to the steep slope of the North Shore; and 2) the occurrence of hard igneous rocks underlying the coastal zone. The fast-running rivers have eroded the softer bedrock to form the deeper parts of the gorges. However, the bedrock has some harder parts, such as dikes or the lower parts of lava flows, and these resist erosion, leading to falls and cascades. Many of the falls on the Cascade River represent individual basalt lava flows.

2.3 (7.2)
CUT LOG CAMPSITE

After SHT crosses a 25-foot bridge, it comes to the Cut Log Campsite. Check out the remains of two very large white pines cut by loggers many years ago and left behind. One of these logs, at the edge of the campsite, is nearly four feet in diameter. SHT continues through the valley of a tributary. Catch some outstanding views of the Cascade River just before the SHT intersects Co. Rd. 45.

▲ CUT LOG CAMPSITE

TYPE: Regular
TENT PADS: 3
WATER: From small creek below campsite
SETTING: 2.1 miles from Cascade River State Park
PREVIOUS CAMPSITE: 0.5 miles
NEXT CAMPSITE: 2.3 miles

3.6 (5.9)
JUNCTION WITH CO. RD. 45

Turn right and follow Co. Rd. 45 0.3 miles to junction with east side trail at parking lot. This ends west side trail. Hikers can now either return to Hwy. 61 on the east side going downstream (right turn) or go on to Bally Creek going upstream.

FOLLOWING EAST SIDE CASCADE RIVER

From bridge above gorgeous waterfalls SHT meets a spur from the state park trailhead and campground. SHT climbs steeply, then levels off. SHT soon turns off of state park hiking/ski trail. At this point, look for short spur to an overlook of the river. SHT descends Trout Creek, crosses bridge and passes campsite.

1.3 (8.2)
CAMPSITE ENTRANCE

SHT follows bluff above river, with occasional views and sounds of the river below. Note how tree mix along river differs from that along bluff.

▲ TROUT CREEK CAMPSITE

TYPE: Regular
TENT PADS: 5
WATER: From Cascade River
SETTING: 1.3 miles from Highway 61, on steep river bank
PREVIOUS CAMPSITE: 3.2 miles
NEXT CAMPSITE: 3.7 miles

3.2 (6.3)
SHT RETURNS TO RIVER

SHT makes steep descent to river's edge, climbs bluff, and makes another steep descent to river (hiking sticks may be helpful, particularly if ground is wet). Note Hidden Falls, a very picturesque area with several good rest spots. SHT continues along Cascade River through cedar, pine, alder and birch.

3.9 (5.6)
CO. RD. 45 AND PARKING LOT

SHT passes under bridge, into parking lot, and continues from left side of lot entrance road, about 100 feet in from Co. Rd. 45. If hiking the Cascade River loop, walk 0.3 miles west (left, across the bridge) on Co. Rd. 45 to the next trailhead sign. This area had a CCC camp in the early 1930s. If continuing on, SHT leads gradually along ridge, descends to cross Minnow Trap Creek and then climbs steps to follow top of bluff along Cascade River. Note views of river and ridges to northwest.

4.6 (4.9)
NORTH CASCADE RIVER CAMPSITE

At campsite spur, SHT turns sharply and moves away from river. SHT climbs gradually, passing through alder thickets, across planks, and through a stand of red pine (whose needles carpet the ground) to reach a ridge overlooking the Sundling Creek valley. Eagle Mountain, the highest point in Minnesota, is visible from here. Note views across valley to north and government survey markers with "bearing trees." SHT descends past a series of cross trails and steps to XC ski trail.

⚠ NORTH CASCADE RIVER CAMPSITE

TYPE: Multi-group
TENT PADS: 6
WATER: From Cascade River
SETTING: 0.7 miles north of Co. Rd. 45
PREVIOUS CAMPSITE: 2.3 miles on west side of Cascade River or 3.7 miles
   on east side of Cascade River
NEXT CAMPSITE: 4.3 miles

6.0 (3.5)
CROSS XC SKI TRAIL

SHT climbs low ridge and follows edge of logged area. Note rapid aspen growth as the quick-growing tree sprouts from runners. SHT then climbs another ridge with views back to Lake Superior. SHT continues along several ridges though mixed forest to a high point on the ridge.

8.4 (1.1)
SPUR TRAIL

Spur goes north 0.7 miles to Bally Creek Rd. (Forest Rd. 158) parking lot. Spur goes through birch forest, crosses a low area, climbs a low ridge and descends to beaver pond on Sundling Creek. Spur crosses creek, then follows a rise into parking lot.

▲ SUNDLING CREEK CAMPSITE

TYPE: Regular
TENT PADS: 4
WATER: From Sundling Creek
SETTING: 0.2 miles from Bally Creek Rd. parking lot on spur trail
PREVIOUS CAMPSITE: 4.3 miles
NEXT CAMPSITE: 1.7 miles

Main SHT continues along ridgeline through hardwoods with many views to north. SHT begins gradual descent through stand of red pine, then descends to Bally Creek Rd. (Forest Rd. 158) parking lot.

9.5 (0.0)
BALLY CREEK RD. TRAILHEAD PARKING LOT

Bally Creek Road to Grand Marais

START (END)
Forest Rd. 158 (Bally Creek Rd.)

END (START)
Pincushion Mountain trailhead north of Grand Marais, Co. Rd. 53 (Pincushion Dr.)

LENGTH OF TRAIL SECTION
8.3 miles

ACCESS AND PARKING
BALLY CREEK ROAD
Nearest Hwy. 61 milepost: 101.7

Secondary Road name and number: Co. Rd. 158 (Bally Creek Rd.)

Turn north on Co. Rd. 7 and follow it approximately 4.3 miles to a dirt road (Co. Rd. 48), then left for 0.3 miles to "T" intersection with Forest Rd. 158. Left on Forest Rd. 158 for 1 mile to spot where main SHT crosses the road. Parking on the left for 4-5 cars. There is additional parking 1.5 miles farther along Forest Rd. 158 with 10–15 parking spaces available.

ACCESS AND PARKING
FOREST RD. 115F
Nearest Hwy 61 milepost: 101.7

Follow Co. Rd. 7 6.0 miles to Co. Rd. 6. Left on Co. Rd. 6 1.5 miles to parking area at intersection of Forest Rd. 115F.

FACILITIES
At starting trailhead: none

Designated campsites on this section of the SHT: Two

SYNOPSIS
The western half of this section is marked by a large beaver pond and Sundling Creek. The SHT passes through a large red pine forest before it joins the North Shore State Trail for 2.5 miles. From west to east this is a particularly nice walk for novice hikers ready for a longer trek.

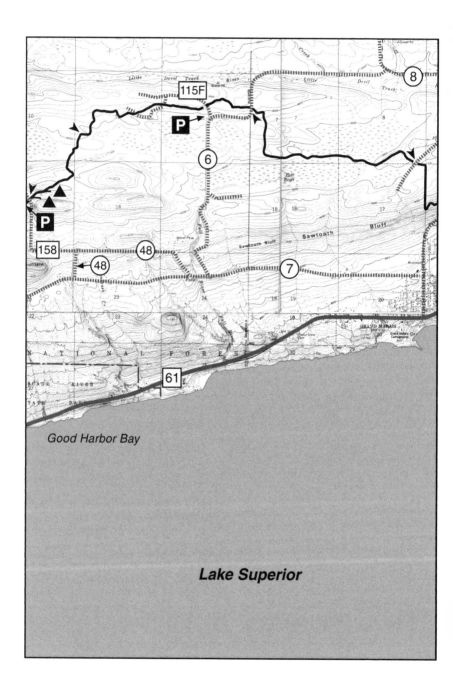

Good Harbor Bay

Lake Superior

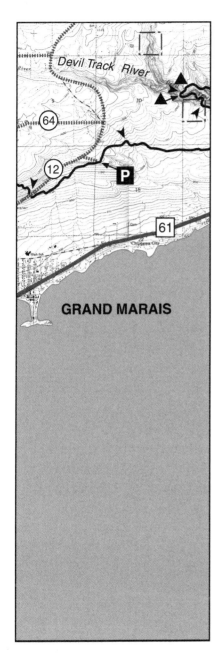

GRAND MARAIS

MILE-BY-MILE DESCRIPTION

0.0 (8.3)
JUNCTION WITH BALLY CREEK ROAD

The first campsite spur is only 0.2 miles into the hike.

▲ SOUTH BALLY CREEK POND CAMPSITE

TYPE: Regular
TENT PADS: 4
WATER: From beaver pond—
   level may be low
SETTING: 0.2 miles from Bally
   Creek Rd., on old beaver pond
PREVIOUS CAMPSITE: 1.7 miles
NEXT CAMPSITE: 0.2 miles

SHT crosses a 13-foot bridge over a small creek that drains the beaver pond and travels along the beaver pond.

▲ NORTH BALLY CREEK POND CAMPSITE

TYPE: Regular
TENT PADS: 3
WATER: From beaver pond
SETTING: 0.3 miles from Bally
   Creek Rd., on old beaver pond
PREVIOUS CAMPSITE: 0.2 miles
NEXT CAMPSITE: 10.5 miles

There is a short climb away from the pond into mixed deciduous forest, then a gradual descent to Sundling Creek through pines. Find a rest bench to the right at Sundling Creek.

0.8 (7.5)
SUNDLING CREEK DAM
SHT follows 193 feet of boardwalk over the beaver dam with a nice view of the creek. Trail ascends back into mixed conifers and aspen. Trail comes to wet area with a 15-foot bridge over a small creek. SHT enters an aspen forest.

2.1 (6.2)
WEST CROSSING OF FOREST RD.
SHT crosses this old forest road three times within a mile. SHT soon enters one of the largest red pine forests on the entire length of the trail, a plantation planted in 1937.

At the easterly of the three crossings, at 3.1(5.2), a spur trail heads 0.1 miles south to Cook Co. Rd. 6 and parking lot. SHT continues east.

3.7 (4.6)
COOK CO. RD. 6 CROSSING
SHT crosses the road and continues 0.2 miles to the North Shore State Trail. SHT follows the North Shore State Trail for the next 2.5 miles. The North Shore State Trail is a wider path used by snowmobiles and the John Beargrease Sled Dog Race in the winter. The joined trail passes through very wet areas and gradually rises to a drier area bordered by mixed forest.

6.3 (2.0)
COOK CO. RD. 64 (TOWER RD.)
The radio and television transmitters are visible to the right. Shortly SHT leaves the North Shore State Trail on right and heads toward Grand Marais with Lake Superior gradually becoming visible. SHT traverses a long wet area on boardwalk. As SHT descends, the Lake becomes more visible. The SHT continues east with a very steep descent and views of Lake Superior.

7.3 (1.0)
GUNFLINT TRAIL (CO. RD. 12) CROSSING
No parking here, but road edge is wide and safe. This is the closest access to Grand Marais for services. SHT crosses road and goes uphill, eventually joining a XC ski trail. SHT continues uphill (downhill

leads to High School football field), crosses the North Shore State Trail and comes to dramatic views at the Pincushion Mountain trailhead.

8.3 (0.0)
PINCUSHION MOUNTAIN TRAILHEAD PARKING LOT

Grand Marais to Cook County Road 58

START (END)
Pincushion Mountain trailhead
parking lot, on Co. Rd. 53
(Pincushion Dr.) just off
Gunflint Trail (Co. Rd. 12)

END (START)
Cook Co. Rd. 58 (Lindskog Rd.)

LENGTH OF TRAIL SECTION
4.9 miles

SAFETY CONCERNS
• Cliffs close to trail edge at
  Devil Track Canyon

• Steep ascent and descent into
  canyon

ACCESS AND PARKING
Nearest Hwy. 61 milepost:
109.3

Secondary road name and number: Gunflint Trail (Co. Rd. 12)

Go north on Gunflint Trail 1.7
miles, then turn east on Co. Rd.
53, 0.25 miles to trailhead.
Turnoff from Gunflint Trail
well-marked as "Scenic
Overlook." Overnight okay.

FACILITIES

At starting trailhead (farthest
southwest): outhouse

Designated campsites on this
section of the SHT: two

SYNOPSIS
This is a 4.9-mile walk with an
optional spur to a panoramic
vista at summit of Pincushion
Mountain. There are side loops
available on the Pincushion Trail
system. The Devil Track River
crossing and the hike on the
canyon edge offer dramatic views
into the canyon gorge.

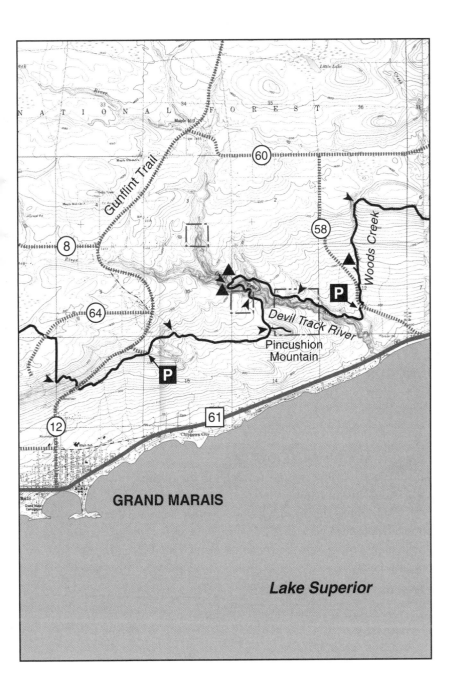

Gunflint Trail

Woods Creek

Little Lake

NATIONAL FOREST

60

58

8

64

Devil Track River

Pincushion
Mountain

P

P

61

12

GRAND MARAIS

Lake Superior

MILE-BY-MILE DESCRIPTION

0.0 (4.9)
PINCUSHION MOUNTAIN TRAILHEAD
This is a popular trailhead for XC skiing, with 25 kilometers of groomed trails. The SHT follows ski trails for 2.2 miles. You must stay off the groomed trails in winter.

0.4 (4.5)
JUNCTION #4
SHT turns right here and travels along ski trail through mixed forest and several small creeks.

1.7 (3.2)
SPUR TRAIL TO PINCUSHION MOUNTAIN SUMMIT
0.25-mile spur trail to summit with sweeping vistas of Grand Marais, Sawtooth Mountains, Lake Superior, and Devil Track River valley.

2.2 (2.7)
JUNCTION OF SKI TRAIL AND SHT
SHT departs ski trail and descends over 200 feet down to Devil Track River along 150 steps.

2.5 (2.4)
DEVIL TRACK RIVER BRIDGE
This 50-foot "A"-shape bridge was built in the summer of 1992. The canyon is deep and remote. Campsites on both west and east side of river. SHT climbs steeply uphill from campsite, about 0.2 miles to Spruce Knob, then continues along canyon's edge, crossing wooden planks at 2.9 and 3.5 miles. Watch for scenic waterfalls and gorgeous red cliffs below.

▲ WEST DEVIL TRACK CAMPSITE

TYPE: Regular
TENT PADS: 6
WATER: From Devil Track River
SETTING: 2.5 miles from Pincushion trailhead, on west bank of river
PREVIOUS CAMPSITE: 10.5 miles
NEXT CAMPSITE: 0.1 miles

▲ EAST DEVIL TRACK CAMPSITE

TYPE: Regular
TENT PADS: 2
WATER: From Devil Track River
SETTING: 2.6 miles from
   Pincushion trailhead, on east
   bank of river
PREVIOUS CAMPSITE: 0.1 miles
NEXT CAMPSITE: 2.9 miles

3.9 (1.0)
BARRIER FALLS OVERLOOK

Deep vista into canyon. SHT passes 1937 tree plantation marker, and eventually descends steps to cross stream on bridge. SHT continues through aspen, birch, and pine. A fisherman's trail crosses the SHT and heads straight down to river. About 0.2 miles from parking lot is the last (or first) good overlook on canyon.

4.9 (0.0)
COOK CO. RD. 58 (LINDSKOG RD.) TRAILHEAD PARKING LOT

CROSS COUNTRY SKIING & THE NORTH SHORE SNOWBELT

At numerous places, the Superior Hiking Trail intersects or shares its route with a cross-country ski trail. Ski trails are wider than the hiking trail, tend to be grassy, and often have blue diamonds marking their course. The winter skier can have an experience similar to that of the summer hiker, with the same beautiful forests, dramatic overlooks and ease of access. There is an extensive network of trails that link all parts of the North Shore. The winter experience is made all the more enjoyable by the generally ample snow, created by the lake-effect snowfall along the North Shore ridgeline. It's not unusual to have two feet of snow inland and none along the highway. Note: if snowshoeing the SHT in winter, please stay off of any groomed ski track.

Cook County Road 58 to Kadunce River Wayside

START (END)
Cook Co. Rd. 58 (Lindskog Rd.)

END (START)
Kadunce River Wayside on
Hwy. 61 (called Kodonce Creek
on highway sign)

LENGTH OF TRAIL SECTION
9.2 miles to Kadunce River
Wayside

6.8 miles to Co. Rd. 14

ACCESS AND PARKING
CO. RD. 58
Nearest Hwy. 61 milepost:
113.8

Secondary road name and
number: Co. Rd. 58

Go north on Co. Rd. 58 0.8
miles to trailhead parking lot.
Overnight okay.

ACCESS AND PARKING
CO. RD. 14
Nearest Hwy. 61 milepost:
117.6

Secondary road name and number: Co. Rd. 14.

Go 0.7 miles from Hwy. 61 to
parking lot. Overnight okay.

FACILITIES
At starting trailhead (farthest
southwest): none

Designated campsites on this
section of the SHT: six

SYNOPSIS
There are a number of unusual
features to this section of the
SHT. The section begins and
ends with intimate streams,
from the gentle gurgle of Woods
Creek to the deep gorges of the
Kadunce River, which offer a
fascinating glimpse into the
region's geology. The middle
part of the section takes you
across a unique high, wet area
with many footbridges. Trees on
this section include oak and
black spruce.

MILE-BY-MILE DESCRIPTION

0.0 (9.2)
PARKING LOT ON CO. RD. 58
SHT crosses Co. Rd. 58 and then follows Woods Creek through birch, aspen and ash. The sharp-edged red rock is rhyolite. SHT then goes through dark spruces with old man's beard (a lichen) drooping from branches.

▲ WOOD'S CREEK CAMPSITE

TYPE: Regular
TENT PADS: 4
WATER: From Woods Creek
SETTING: 0.6 miles east of Co. Rd. 58, on creek
PREVIOUS CAMPSITE: 2.9 miles
NEXT CAMPSITE: 2.4 miles

1.2 (8.0)
SHT LEAVES CREEK
SHT turns east and climbs into parklike aspen and birch forest, then a series of logged areas and nice open field (SHT marked by rock cairns). Views of Lake Superior, Pincushion Mountain at first, then wide view southwest of Pincushion, Maple Hill radio tower, and Sawtooth range. Birches gradually give way to aspens. In the open area, watch for bluebirds in the field and Five-Mile Rock in Lake Superior. At far side of field, SHT enters a mixed woods, crosses an ATV trail, passes through a wildlife opening, and then goes through a spruce plantation.

3.0 (6.2)
DURFEE CREEK CAMPSITE
After campsite, SHT crosses a series of plank bridges in this up-and-down section, with lots of white spruce and old burned stumps.

⚠ DURFEE CREEK CAMPSITE

TYPE: Multi-group
TENT PADS: 6
WATER: From Durfee Creek
SETTING: 3.0 miles east of Co. Rd. 58
PREVIOUS CAMPSITE: 2.4 miles
NEXT CAMPSITE: 1.1 miles

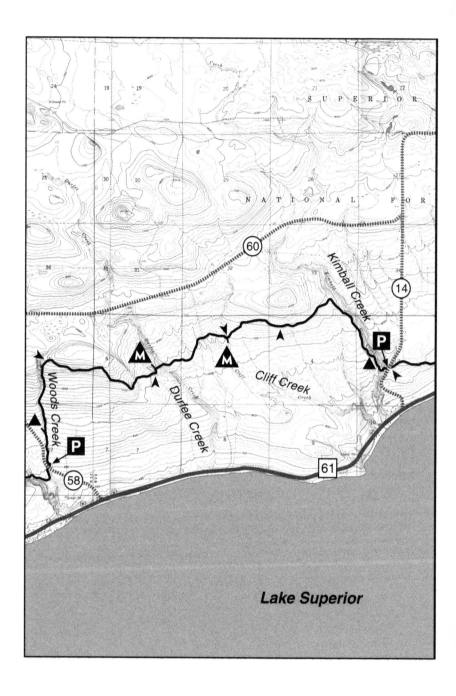

Lake Superior

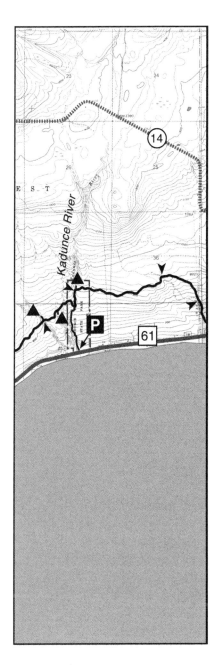

4.1 (5.1)
CLIFF CREEK CROSSING
Woods become more mixed, with birch, aspen and fir. Lake Superior comes into view, the sharp, red rhyolite returns underfoot, and there are occasional vistas.

⚠ CLIFF CREEK CAMPSITE

TYPE: Multi-group
TENT PADS: 8
WATER: From Cliff Creek
SETTING: 2.7 miles west of
   Co. Rd. 14
PREVIOUS CAMPSITE: 1.1 miles
NEXT CAMPSITE: 2.6 miles

5.1 (4.1)
SCRUB-OAK OVERLOOK
Expansive view of Lake Superior. On SHT look for the unusual small oak trees in field and large (30-inch diameter) aspens. SHT begins to follow Kimball Creek in a towering cedar forest, crosses the creek, and crosses the Kimball Creek Trail (an unmaintained fishing trail along the river). SHT then crosses a small tributary and climbs steep steps. The bridge on Kimball Creek is one of the most picturesque settings on the trail.

▲ KIMBALL CREEK CAMPSITE

TYPE: Regular
TENT PADS: 3
WATER: From Kimball Creek
SETTING: 0.1 mile west of
   Co. Rd. 14, at base of hill
PREVIOUS CAMPSITE: 2.6 miles
NEXT CAMPSITE: 1.2 miles

6.8 (2.4)
COOK CO. RD. 14

SHT crosses road at parking lot and climbs through cutover area, then passes under powerline before entering a spruce/fir/birch/ aspen woods. After a view of Lake Superior, SHT descends. Look for bunchberry and thimbleberry. SHT crosses a couple of footpaths and a small opening. Trail is mostly rock here. SHT descends stone steps to Crow Creek.

▲ CROW CREEK CAMPSITE

TYPE: Regular
TENT PADS: 4
WATER: From Crow Creek
SETTING: 1.3 miles east of Co. Rd. 14
PREVIOUS CAMPSITE: 1.2 miles
NEXT CAMPSITE: 0.4 miles

7.9 (1.3)
CROW CREEK

This stream has the steep rock walls typical of Kadunce River visible upstream from the bridge. SHT climbs out of creek drainage, crosses a footpath, then comes to another narrow steep canyon, the west fork of the Kadunce River. Watch for bearing tree near SHT right before crossing.

▲ WEST FORK OF THE KADUNCE CAMPSITE

TYPE: Regular
TENT PADS: 4
WATER: Stream is mostly dry and hard to get to; use Kadunce River (0.5 miles)
SETTING: 1.5 miles east of Co. Rd. 14
PREVIOUS CAMPSITE: 0.4 miles
NEXT CAMPSITE: 0.5 miles

8.5 (0.7)
KADUNCE RIVER

On far side of bridge, go downstream on spectacular spur trail 0.7 miles to Hwy. 61. Spur follows river until river drops into gorge, then rejoins river after gorge. The canyon is very deep yet only about eight feet wide in places.

9.2 (0.0)
KADUNCE RIVER WAYSIDE ON HWY. 61

PEBBLE BEACHES

A beach must have both a source of rock particles and wave action to deposit and move the particles. Beaches continually change in reaction to changes in the waves from storm to calm to storm. Some of the smaller beaches on the North Shore are made of rocks ripped from the nearby bedrock ledges; larger beaches are made possible where the waves have access to more easily-eroded glacial deposits. The long, low beaches between Grand Marais and Hovland are made both from local volcanic rhyolite, which breaks up into easily erodible chips or shingles, and reworked older beach deposits from the Nipissing stage of Lake Superior, about 5000 years ago, when the lake was slightly higher and the beaches were on the other side of what is now the highway. Can you find any agates? They might have been brought by the ice sheet from Isle Royale or Canada.

Kadunce River Wayside to Judge Magney State Park

START (END)
Kadunce River Wayside on Hwy. 61 (called Kodonce Creek on highway sign)

END (START)
Judge C.R. Magney State Park

LENGTH OF TRAIL SECTION
10.0 miles

SAFETY CONCERNS
• Trail near cliff edge at times along Kadunce River

ACCESS AND PARKING
KADUNCE RIVER
Nearest Hwy. 61 milepost: 119

Secondary road name and number: none

Parking at Wayside: 11 spaces available, no overnight

ACCESS AND PARKING
LAKEWALK
Nearest Hwy. 61 milepost: 120.2 at west end, 121.6 at east end

Secondary road name and number: none

Parking available off highway, no parking lot

FACILITIES
At starting trailhead (farthest southwest): none

Designated campsites on this section of trail: four

SYNOPSIS
This is an exciting section of the SHT, since it is the only part which is directly on the Lake Superior shoreline. It also passes through many different stages of tree succession following logging in the area, and some classic North Shore river gorges, including the Kadunce River.

0.0 (10.0)
KADUNCE RIVER WAYSIDE

This spectacular 0.7-mile spur trail begins climbing almost immediately along the edge of the Kadunce River gorge, which is pocked by occasional "swirl caves" created at various stages of the gorge's creation. Spur trail meets the main SHT at bridge crossing the Kadunce River.

0.7 (9.3)
BRIDGE OVER KADUNCE RIVER

Spur trail joins main SHT here. SHT turns away from bridge, climbs hill and follows river upstream past cascades, then climbs again and leaves river. Forest changes from birch and fir to dense, relatively younger aspen. SHT crosses an old grassy logging roadbed and then two footpaths.

▲ KADUNCE RIVER CAMPSITE

TYPE: Regular
TENT PADS: 3
WATER: From Kadunce River
SETTING: 0.9 miles from Hwy. 61.
PREVIOUS CAMPSITE: 0.5 miles
NEXT CAMPSITE: 5.3 miles

2.0 (8.0)
BLUEBERRY OVERLOOK

Follow rock cairns through open area that leads to overlook with expansive view of Lake Superior. SHT crosses stream and enters mixed woods. SHT then enters another logged area replanted with spruce, with large white pines left standing. SHT descends and passes many raspberry patches in a young aspen forest.

2.7 (7.3)
KELLY'S HILL ROAD

SHT crosses road (note SHT mileage sign), then descends through scrubby woods, dense young aspen stand and mixed woods.

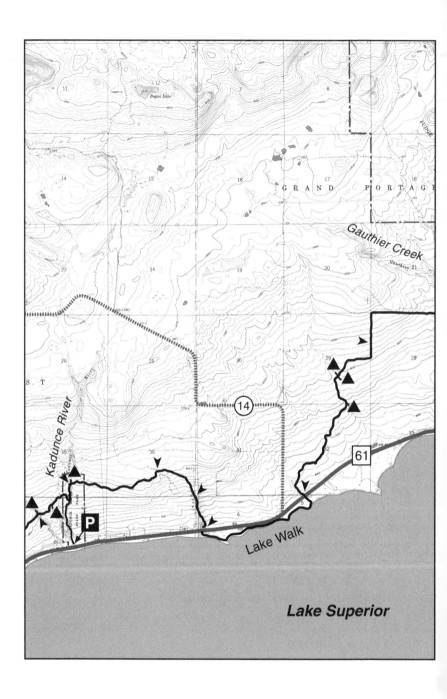

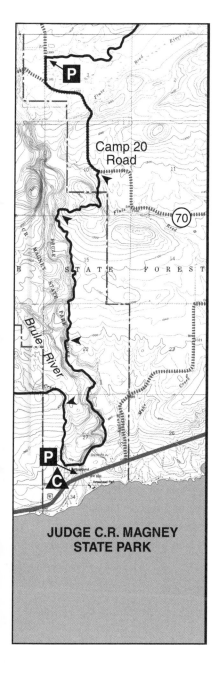

3.2 (6.8)
HWY. 61, WEST END OF LAKEWALK

SHT is marked on both sides of Hwy. 61. SHT follows shore of Lake Superior on a soft pebble beach. This is the only part of the SHT on Lake Superior. Here one can literally touch the many moods of this great lake. Notice the different surge levels up the beach from storms and wind, especially the unimpeded northeast winds. Look for bog areas between beach and Hwy. 61— good spring birding, as birds use shoreline for navigation. SHT turns inland just past a very small rock island barely off shore.

4.8 (5.2)
HWY. 61, EAST END OF LAKEWALK

After crossing Hwy. 61, SHT passes large birches and passes under powerline and through mixed woods along Hane Creek. Cross stream on small wood bridge after passing through low areas. SHT eventually climbs and passes large cedar and white pine and overlooks of waterfalls and pools on Little Brule River. SHT crosses river on log planking, ascends through mature aspen, then levels out.

▲ SOUTH LITTLE BRULE RIVER CAMPSITE

TYPE: Regular
TENT PADS: 2
WATER: From Little Brule River
SETTING: 1.5 miles from Hwy. 61
PREVIOUS CAMPSITE: 5.3 miles
NEXT CAMPSITE: 0.4 miles

▲ NORTH LITTLE BRULE RIVER CAMPSITE

TYPE: Regular
TENT PADS: 4
WATER: From Little Brule River
SETTING: 1.9 miles from Hwy. 61
PREVIOUS CAMPSITE: 0.4 miles
NEXT CAMPSITE: 0.0 miles

▲ NORTHWEST LITTLE BRULE RIVER CAMPSITE

TYPE: Regular
TENT PADS: 3
WATER: From Little Brule River
SETTING: 1.9 miles from Hwy. 61
PREVIOUS CAMPSITE: 0.0 miles
NEXT CAMPSITE: 11.9 miles
   (or use Judge C.R. Magney State Park)

7.1 (2.9)
GRAVEL PIT ROAD

SHT winds through young aspen forest. Look for blueberries in open sections. For approximately 1.5 miles the SHT follows the straight borderline of private property, past Lake Superior views and mature pines. SHT crosses old road bed upon exiting another section of private land and shortly passes bearing tree and survey line, then follows Gauthier Creek.

9.1 (0.9)
JUNCTION WITH STATE PARK TRAIL

As the trail begins to leave from Gauthier Creek, SHT joins state park ski trail and continues to parking lot.

10.0 (0.0)
JUDGE C.R. MAGNEY STATE PARK TRAILHEAD

SHT enters parking lot located just north of state park campground.

Judge Magney State Park to County Road 70

START (END)
Judge Magney State Park
Parking Lot

END (START)
Parking Lot on Co. Rd. 70
(Camp 20 Road)

LENGTH OF TRAIL SECTION
6.6 miles

ACCESS AND PARKING
Nearest Hwy 61 milepost:
123.8

State park permit needed.
Overnight okay, register vehicle
at contact station

FACILITIES
At starting trailhead: Pit toilet,
drinking water, picnic tables,
campground

Designated Campsites on this
section: none; Judge Magney
State Park has 36 fee campsites

SYNOPSIS
In this section, the trail follows
the Brule River for over two
miles and features the dramatic
Devil's Kettle Falls. The trail
continues through mixed forest
with occasional large cedars and
white pine on the high bluff
above the Brule River. The trail
climbs to a rocky knob with a
view of Lake Superior then
descends into the picturesque
Flute Reed River valley.

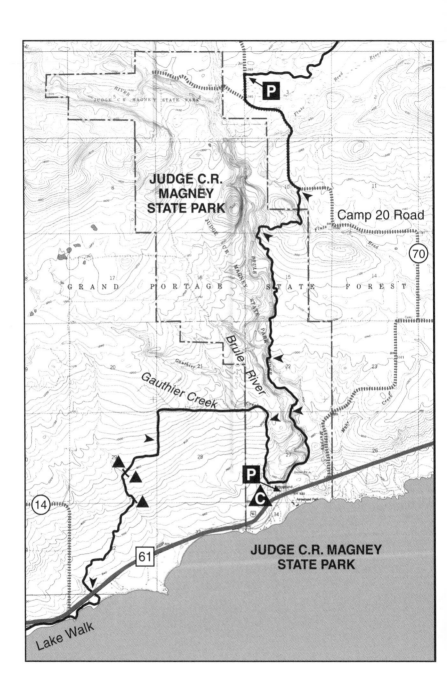

0.0 (6.6)
JUDGE MAGNEY STATE PARK PARKING LOT
SHT goes east (to the right) out of parking lot and crosses the Brule River on a 76-foot bridge by picnic tables and pit toilet. Trail continues on bluff along Brule River with occasional dramatic overlooks and views of Lower and Upper Falls.

1.0 (5.6)
DEVIL'S KETTLE FALLS
SHT goes to overlook of Devil's Kettle Falls, one of the most dramatic falls on trail. Trail continues upstream along the river through beautiful forest of white pine, cedar, balsam fir, birch, spruce and aspen. Watch for occasional blackened tree stumps and cut stumps showing past history of forest.

2.0 (4.6)
SHT LEAVES BRULE RIVER
SHT leaves Brule River at the bottom of a hill with two benches and continues through forest on high bluff parallel to river.

2.8 (3.8)
LARGE WHITE PINE
Look for large white pine on right and occasional large white pine scattered throughout the forest.

JUDGE C.R. MAGNEY STATE PARK

Judge C.R. Magney State Park is named after the former Minnesota Supreme Court Justice Clarence R. Magney. A strong advocate of Minnesota state parks, he was instrumental in establishing eleven parks and waysides along the North Shore. This park was established in 1957 to preserve three waterfalls on the Brule River: the Lower Falls, the Upper Falls, and the Devil's Kettle. The Devil's Kettle was named appropriately. A large rock juts out and splits the river in two. The east branch drops 50 feet to a deep gorge and pool. The west branch plunges into a huge pothole and, according to legend, disappears forever. 4,674 acres in size, today the park has nine miles of trail and 36 campsites.

3.9 (2.7)
ROCKY KNOB
SHT climbs to rocky knob covered with reindeer lichen. Look for views of Lake Superior. Trail continues along rocky outcrops. Watch for cairns marking trail. Trail crosses a private road—please stay on trail. The trail descends steeply and travels on private land through alder, ash, aspen and balsam forest.

4.8 (1.8)
FLUTE REED RIVER BRIDGE
SHT crosses Flute Reed River, still on private land, and continues 300 feet to Co. Rd. 70 (Camp 20 Rd.). Trail continues on Co. Rd. 70 (Camp 20 Rd.) 1.7 miles north to parking lot. Note: Okay to park on the south side of Co. Rd. 70 (Camp 20 Rd.) by the Flute Reed River bridge for day hikes only. No overnight parking here.

6.6 (0.0)
TRAILHEAD PARKING LOT ON CAMP 20 ROAD
Absolutely no parking on road if parking lot is full. There is heavy truck traffic on this road.

County Road 70 to Arrowhead Trail

START (END)
Co. Rd. 70 (Camp 20 Rd.)

END (START)
Co. Rd. 16 (Arrowhead Trail)

LENGTH OF TRAIL SECTION
8.5 miles

ACCESS AND PARKING
Nearest Hwy. 61 milepost:
124.4

From Hwy. 61, turn north on
Co. Rd. 69 (North Rd.) and go
2.75 miles. Turn north (left) on
Co. Rd. 70 (Camp 20 Rd.) and
follow road 4.75 miles to trailhead parking lot on right side of
road (about 0.25 miles past
Hong Hill Rd. sign on left side
of road)

Room for six cars, overnight
okay. Absolutely no parking on
road outside of parking lot.

FACILITIES
At starting trailhead: none

Designated campsites on this
section of the SHT: three

SYNOPSIS
This section is in the Flute Reed
and Carlson Creek watersheds.
The large number of ponds
along the SHT make it ideal for
wildlife viewing, including
waterfowl, beaver, and moose.
There is a good deal of past and
current beaver activity. The trail
also travels though a young tree
plantation with additional
wildlife viewing opportunities.

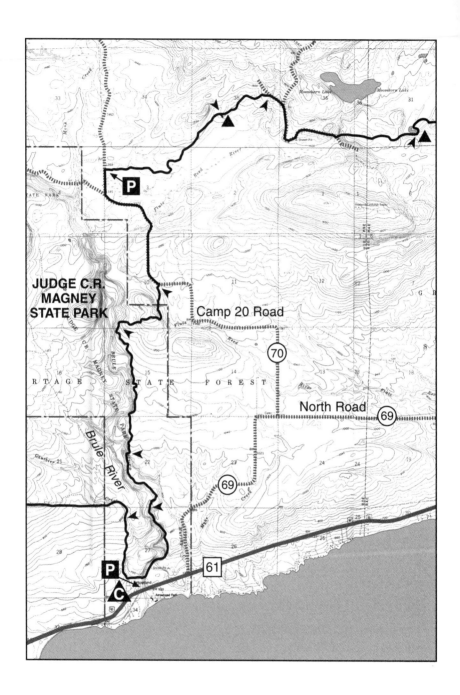

JUDGE C.R.
MAGNEY
STATE PARK

Camp 20 Road

North Road

Brule River

P

C

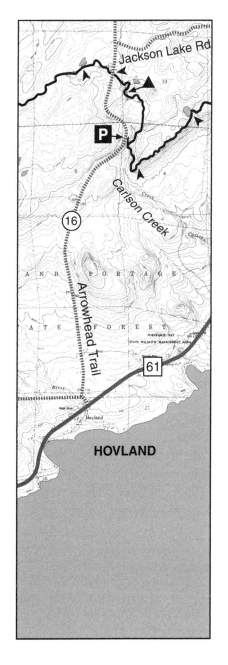

0.0 (8.5)
CO. RD. 70 (CAMP 20 RD.)
TRAILHEAD PARKING LOT

Absolutely no parking on Camp 20 Rd. due to heavy equipment use of narrow road. SHT leaves parking lot and continues for 1.3 miles on private land. The first 0.25 miles is a mix of balsam poplar (also called Balm-of-Gilead), black ash, and tag alder. Trail comes into clearing where forest has been clearcut and replanted with spruce, white pine, and cedar so please stay on trail at all times. SHT passes islands of mature spruce among planted trees. Watch for moose sign. Trail crosses two branches of Flute Reed River and also has nice view of pond where moose may occasionally be seen.

Note: If staying at the Hazel Campsite, second Flute Reed tributary crossing is water source for the campsite that is 1.8 miles farther on.

1.3 (7.2)
HAZEL CORRIDOR

SHT leaves private land and travels through a corridor of mixed forest with hazel predominating.

2.2 (6.3)
HAZEL CAMPSITE

▲ HAZEL CAMPSITE
_____

TYPE: REGULAR
TENT PADS: 3
WATER: none (there may be a potential water source at tiny
   creek by curved ash tree 0.25 miles before camp site but
   don't rely on it). Get water from Flute Reed River branch,
   1.8 miles before campsite
SETTING: 2.2 miles from trailhead
PREVIOUS CAMPSITE: 11.9 miles; or 8.8 miles from Judge
   Magney State Park Campground
NEXT CAMPSITE: 3.0 miles

SHT continues through mixed forest of spruce, birch, balsam, aspen, alder, and ash. The trail rises steeply on an old roadbed just before the Tom Lake Rd. and trailhead sign.

2.6 (5.9)
TOM LAKE RD.
SHT continues on Tom Lake Rd. to east (right) for 1.3 miles. Numerous big white pine along road. Dog sledders also train along this road. Boyd Rd. is on left about 0.25 miles past trailhead sign. Moosehorn Lake Rd. is on the left 0.8 miles further on. Trail/road continues for another 0.25 miles then turns sharply uphill (left) at white pine ridge. Watch for trailhead sign. SHT ascends hill on steep steps. Trail continues on hilltop through moss-covered blown-down trees. Note evidence of past fire in area. Trail continues through young sugar maple forest and then descends into birch, balsam, spruce, and aspen forest.

5.1 (3.4)
CARLSON POND
SHT comes to Carlson Pond, a 200-300 acre beaver pond with two lobes. Balsam and spruce covered islands dot pond. Watch for moose feeding in the pond. SHT continues along first lobe of pond, crosses Carlson Creek below pond on split log bridge and reaches second lobe.

▲ SOUTH CARLSON POND CAMPSITE

TYPE: Regular
TENT PADS: 6
WATER: From Carlson Pond
SETTING: On Carlson Pond
PREVIOUS CAMPSITE: 3.0 miles
NEXT CAMPSITE: 2.3 miles

SHT leaves pond and goes through mixed spruce, balsam, aspen, birch forest with occasional glimpses of ponds spread out along Carlson Creek. Trail comes to large pond by a large spruce tree, a nice rest stop. Look for moose sign. Trail continues through mixed forest with boardwalk in some areas.

6.5 (2.0)
OLD BEAVER POND

SHT crosses by old beaver pond and continues through mixed forest. Trail goes through red pine plantation and then along Carlson Creek until it reaches Co. Rd. 16 (Arrowhead Trail).

6.9 (1.6)
CO. RD. 16 (ARROWHEAD TRAIL) CROSSING

SHT continues on other side of road. No parking facilities here. SHT continues along Carlson Creek and comes to a large beaver pond. Note the huge 24-inch diameter aspen cut by beaver at campsite entrance.

7.4 (1.1)
NORTH CARLSON POND CAMPSITE

▲ NORTH CARLSON POND CAMPSITE

TYPE: Regular
TENT PADS: 6
WATER: From Carlson Creek/Pond
SETTING: 1.1 miles from Co Rd 16 (Arrowhead Trail) trailhead
PREVIOUS CAMPSITE: 2.3 miles
NEXT CAMPSITE: 4.1 miles

SHT continues by Carlson Creek through ash, aspen and alder forest and comes to huge spruce tree. After spruce tree, trail ascends hill and continues through mixed forest. Trail crosses drainage and travels along ridge through balsam fir blowdown area. SHT descends steeply and goes along creek again to Carlson Creek bridge. Spur trail on other side of bridge goes steeply uphill to trailhead parking lot on Co. Rd. 16 (Arrowhead Trail). Main trail does not cross bridge and continues along creek.

8.5 (0.0)
CO. RD. 16 (ARROWHEAD TRAIL) PARKING LOT

Arrowhead Trail to Jackson Lake Road

START (END)
Cook Co. Rd. 16 (Arrowhead Trail) north of Hovland

END (START)
Jackson Lake Rd.

LENGTH OF TRAIL SECTION
5.1 miles

SAFETY CONCERNS
• Blowdowns in spruce-fir forests may obscure the trail

ACCESS AND PARKING
Nearest Hwy. 61 milepost: 128.9

Secondary road name and number: Cook Co. Rd. 16 (Arrowhead Trail)

Follow Arrowhead Trail north 3.3 miles. Trailhead parking lot is on right. Overnight okay.

FACILITIES
At starting trailhead: none

Designated campsites on this section of the SHT: one

SYNOPSIS
This section is home to the ghost of the woodland caribou. Moss-covered rocks and lichen-draped trees give this land a true boreal feel. Experience the variety as the SHT winds from open rocky ridges with wide views of Lake Superior and Isle Royale into dark forests and quiet backwaters. One-half of this section follows an open rocky ridge with nearly continuous views.

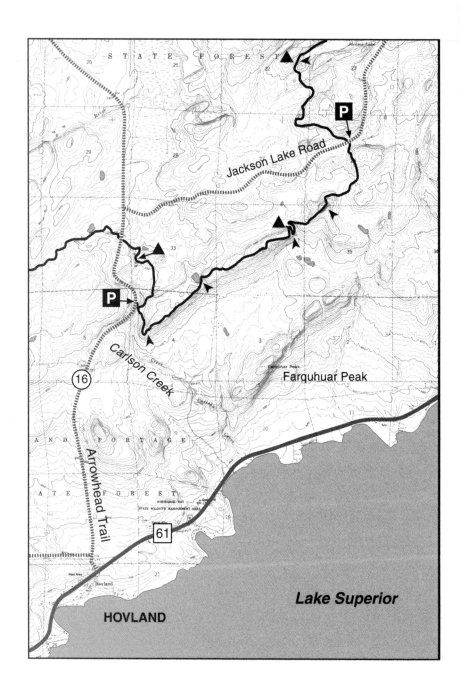

Farquhuar Peak

Carlson Creek

Jackson Lake Road

Lake Superior

HOVLAND

MILE-BY-MILE DESCRIPTION

0.0 (5.1)
PARKING LOT ON ARROWHEAD TRAIL
SHT departs from lot and descends steeply on steps to Carlson Creek. SHT crosses creek on 23-foot bridge and continues along creek through alder before climbing steeply and continuing through large lichen-draped spruce.

0.6 (4.5)
SOUTHWEST END OF RIDGETOP
From the first view through some young aspens, SHT meanders along this ridgeline for 1.5 miles. Cairns lead the way through mixed spruce, fir, and aspen forest as the views keep getting better. Look for Isle Royale over 20 miles away. Watch for beaver meadow as SHT nears a creek.

1.6 (3.5)
CREEK CROSSING
This is a small creek, crossed on a large dead tree. SHT skirts east edge of beaver meadow, then climbs back to ridgetop through dead and dying fir. SHT descends steeply from ridge into a valley, with nice views of beaver pond and Lake Superior below. SHT enters a dark forest, once the habitat of the woodland caribou, before meeting unnamed creek where the water appears to caress moss-covered boulders.

▲ WOODLAND CARIBOU POND CAMPSITE

TYPE: Regular
TENT PADS: 4
WATER: From beaver pond
SETTING: 3.0 miles east of Arrowhead Trail
PREVIOUS CAMPSITE: 4.0 miles
NEXT CAMPSITE: 3.8 miles

3.2 (1.9)
CREEK CROSSING
SHT crosses creek on a split-log footbridge, near a couple of black ash, then climbs east side of creek and follows the edge of beaver meadow. SHT climbs through a relatively mature mixed birch forest.

FIRE ECOLOGY

Forest fires, either by their absence or raging presence, have had significant impact on the forests of the North Shore. Fire is a natural part of many ecosystems, providing a periodic cleansing and an easy way to return nutrients to the soil. Many of the birch forests along the SHT grew up following large-scale forest fires that followed logging in the area—as evidence, look in the even-aged birch forests for the numerous large fire-charred stumps of white pines. The few remaining patches of old-growth pines have likely survived a number of fires with their thick, corky bark and out-of-reach branches.

3.9 (1.2)
HELLACIOUS OVERLOOK
Steep climb rewards hikers with a wide view of Lake Superior, Isle Royale, and beaver meadows below. SHT continues along ridgetop, with more views to the northeast, then descends steeply past dead and dying fir, into a wet area with alder and ash. SHT gradually climbs through aspen, birch and diseased fir, then descends steeply into a cedar swamp and across a corduroy walkway to the road.

5.1 (0.0)
JACKSON LAKE RD. PARKING LOT

Jackson Lake Road to Otter Lake Road

START (END)
Jackson Lake Rd.

END (START)
Otter Lake Rd.

LENGTH OF TRAIL SECTION
8.7 miles

SAFETY CONCERNS
• Tall grass and infrequent marking in places

ACCESS AND PARKING
WEST END
Nearest Hwy. 61 milepost: 128.9

Secondary road names and number: Cook Co. Rd. 16 (Arrowhead Trail), Jackson Lake Rd.

Follow Arrowhead Trail from Hwy. 61 4.5 miles to Jackson Lake Rd. Right on Jackson Lake Rd. 3.1 miles to parking lot.

ACCESS AND PARKING
END OF TRAIL
Follow Arrowhead Trail from Hwy. 61 4.5 miles to Jackson Lake Rd. Turn right on Jackson Lake Rd. and go 8.4 miles to Otter Lake Rd. at "T" intersection. Turn left (west) on Otter Lake Rd. and go 2.0 miles to trailhead parking lot.

FACILITIES
At starting trailhead: none

At ending trailhead: outhouse at Swamp River Public Access site and campsite (just past parking lot)

Designated campsites on this section of the SHT: two

SYNOPSIS
This is the northernmost section of the trail. It connects with the Border Route Trail at the Swamp River. The SHT reaches its highest elevation, 1,829 feet, on this section. Overlooks of Jackson Lake and the Swamp River drainage, and a spectacular maple forest on Sugarbush Ridge, are highlights. This is remote country, yet with significant logging influence in the northern half, it is also not wilderness.

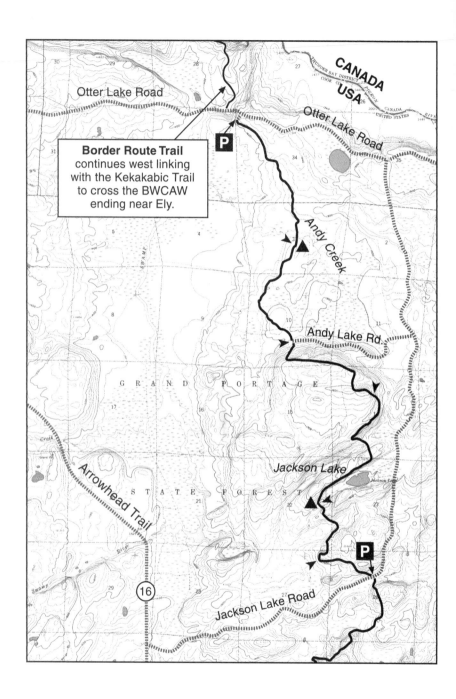

Border Route Trail continues west linking with the Kekakabic Trail to cross the BWCAW ending near Ely.

MILE-BY-MILE DESCRIPTION

0.0 (8.7)
JACKSON LAKE ROAD
The SHT departs from Jackson Lake Rd. The trail heads generally westward past 1997 logging area to the first of several overlooks. The trail goes through mixed aspen, birch, spruce, and sugar maple with large cedar pockets.

0.8 (7.9)
JACKSON CREEK AREA OVERLOOK
The view westward encompasses the Jackson Creek branch of the Swamp River watershed. From here the trail heads northeastward, staying high on the ridge. A glimpse of a small pond through the trees signals the beginning of the descent to a small stream. Hop across the stream on small boulders. The trail continues northward through rolling terrain to the campsite and log bridge on Jackson Creek.

1.7 (7.0)
JACKSON CREEK BRIDGE AND CAMPSITE
Jackson Creek is small but dependable. Just downstream from the bridge is a pool approximately three feet deep. Cool off with a dip. Upstream from the bridge is the site of an old beaver pond, now largely drained, with a picturesque bedrock island within the pond. From Jackson Creek SHT continues around a swampy area before heading uphill and eastward to several partial overlooks above Jackson Lake. SHT drops off from the Jackson Lake Ridge into a cedar forest on the valley floor. It then climbs upward through a beautiful old growth maple forest to several bedrock outcroppings on the eastern face of the SHT's highest hill. Before reaching the high point, SHT turns onto the north slope of the hill, then climbs steeply to the summit plateau.

▲ JACKSON CREEK CAMPSITE

TYPE: Regular
TENT PADS: 3
WATER: From Jackson Creek
SETTING: 1.7 miles from Jackson Lake Rd.
PREVIOUS CAMPSITE: 3.8 miles
NEXT CAMPSITE: 5.3 miles

3.8 (4.9)
HIGHEST POINT OF TRAIL, ROSEBUSH RIDGE
The high point, 1,829 feet, is in the midst of a mixed forest. Watch for sign on tree. There is no view. Continuing west along the summit plateau, views northward can be glimpsed through the trees. Raspberries grow profusely in this area. (The name Rosebush Ridge appears on some maps—apparently because an explorer was torn by thorns and did not properly identify the culprit species.) The SHT descends steeply down to Andy Lake Rd.

5.3 (3.4)
ANDY LAKE ROAD
The final section of trail from Andy Lake Rd. to Otter Lake Rd. is predominantly flat. Andy Lake Rd. is gated so there is no vehicle access. It passes through logged-over areas as well as open meadows of older logged areas. There are also pockets of large cedar throughout.

7.0 (1.7)
ANDY CREEK CAMPSITE AND BRIDGE
The SHT may be hard to follow if not recently weed-whipped in the meadow areas. If so, look for cut ends of trees and treadway through grass. SHT follows mostly old logging roads to the Otter Lake Rd.

▲ ANDY CREEK CAMPSITE

TYPE: Regular
TENT PADS: 4
WATER: From Andy Creek
SETTING: 1.7 miles south of Otter Lake Rd.
PREVIOUS CAMPSITE: 5.3 miles

8.7 (0.0) OTTER LAKE RD. TRAILHEAD PARKING LOT
This is the northern terminus of the Superior Hiking Trail. There is a public access site and campsite on the Swamp River about 300 feet west along the road.

To continue to the Border Route Trail, go 0.2 miles west on the Otter Lake Road to the trailhead for the Border Route Trail.

Information on the Border Route Trail and the Kekekabic Trail

A short side trip on the Border Route Trail is recommended. One mile northward on the Border Route Trail is a wonderful overlook. Below lies the confluence of the Swamp and Pigeon Rivers. Northward is a view encompassing miles of Canadian wilderness. Southward is a great view of the broad Swamp River Valley. Eastward hills march into the distance. Somewhere out there lies Lake Superior.

The Border Route Trail follows the Canadian border, usually high on ridges overlooking lakes and streams as much as 500 feet below. After the first 12 miles, to McFarland Lake, the trail is within the Boundary Waters Canoe Area Wilderness (BWCAW). Federal rules and regulations apply. Permits are required for hiking in the BWCAW portion. From where the SHT meets the Border Route at the Swamp River, the BRT heads west for 65.4 miles to the Gunflint Trail and the nearby eastern trailhead of the Kekekabic Trail. The "Kek" slices through the heart of the BWCAW for 40 miles terminating near Snowbank Lake on the Fernberg Rd. outside of Ely.

The Border Route Trail can be used in conjunction with the SHT for some truly wild hiking experiences. In general, the Border Route is more rugged and less well maintained. Expect to use your maps, guidebook and compass.

The guidebook *The Border Route Trail—A Trail Guide and Map,* by Marcia Scott and Chuck Hoffman, is available from the SHT store or direct from the Minnesota Rovers Outing Club, P. O. Box 14133, Dinkytown Station, Minneapolis, MN 55414.

The Kekekabic Trail guidebook, *The Hiker's BWCA Wilderness Companion: Kekekabic Trail Guide,* by Martin Kubic and Angela Anderson, is also available from the SHT store or direct from the Kekekabic Trail Club, c/o Midwest Mountaineering, 309 Cedar Ave., Minneapolis, MN 55454.

Additional Information

EMERGENCIES
911 in both counties

MAIL
Hiker's mail should be marked "General Delivery—Hold for hiker on Superior Hiking Trail." Post office hours vary.

INFORMATION
• Superior Hiking Trail Association (Store and Office)
PO Box 4, 731 Seventh Ave. (Hwy 61), Two Harbors, MN 55616
tel (218) 834-2700, fax (218) 834-4436, e-mail suphike@mr.net
www.shta.org

• Superior Shuttle
Runs Fridays, Saturdays, Sundays mid-May to Mid-October
stopping at most trailheads twice a day on a fixed schedule
For information and reservations call (218) 834-5511
www.superiorshuttle.com

• North Country Trail Association
229 E. Main Street
Lowell, MI 49331
1-888-454-6282 www.northcountrytrail.org

• H.T. Leasing LTD. (Regular bus service along the North Shore)
Happy Time Tours, 1475 West Walsh St., Thunder Bay, Ontario,
Canada, P7E 4X6 (807) 473-5955
www.httours.com/transportation

• Lodge to Lodge Hiking Program: Boundary Country Trekking
(800) 322-8327 www.boundarycountry.com

• Minnesota State Parks
Information: (888) 646-6367
Reservations: (866) 85 PARKS
www.dnr.state.mn.us/state_parks/

- R.J. Houle Visitor Information Center for Lake County
  1330 Hwy. 61, Two Harbors, MN 55616
  (800) 554-2116 or (218) 834-4005

- Grand Marais Visitor Center, Grand Marais, MN
  (888) 922-5000 or (218) 387-2524

- U.S. Forest Service:
  Tofte Ranger Station (218) 663-8060
  Grand Marais Ranger Station (Gunflint Ranger District)
  (218) 387-1750

One More Nice Day Hike

THERE IS ONE MORE NICE DAY HIKE on the Superior Hiking Trail near Knife River, about five miles southwest of Two Harbors. This 4.2 mile trail section was built in anticipation that the Superior Hiking Trail might one day go through here. It's a very nice hike along the gorgeous Knife River. The trail alternates between pine-studded high banks and riverside stretches.

You can start or end the hike on Scenic Hwy. 61. From Hwy. 61 milepost 18.2 turn east (right) on Co. Rd. 103 (Knife River Rd.). Go 0.3 miles to Scenic Hwy. 61. Turn southwest (right) and go 0.25 miles to parking lot past the bridge on the river.

The trail follows the river for 0.5 miles until it comes to the Hwy. 61 Expressway. Go under the Hwy. 61 bridge, then follow the trail up the bank and onto the shoulder of Hwy. 61, cross the river on the shoulder, and then follow the trail down the bank to the river once more. The trail follows the river about two miles with several nice waterfalls and beautiful stands of red and white pine.

After leaving the river, the trail goes through an aspen-dominated forest for about 0.5 miles until it ends at the Hawk Hill Road trailhead parking lot.

You could start the hike at this trailhead parking lot as well. From Hwy. 61 milepost 18, turn north (left) and go 0.8 miles on Co. Rd. 102 (Hawk Hill Rd.) to the parking lot on the left.

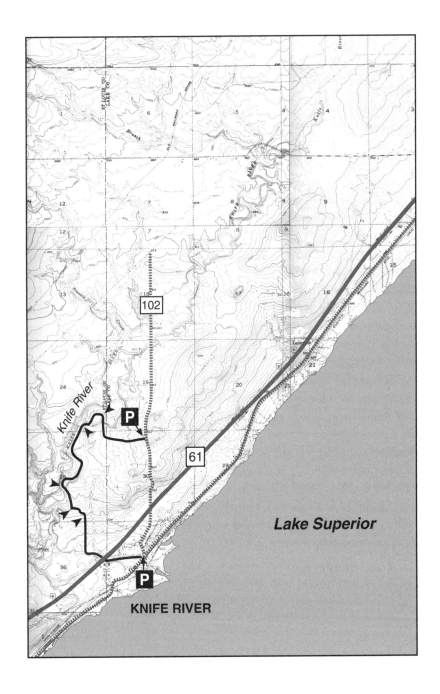

Lake Superior

102

61

KNIFE RIVER

A Final Note

The trouble is, we're tempted to think that a guided description can really describe and guide. Of course, no matter how well done, it cannot. It depends on what we're looking for.

The Superior Hiking Trail leads us from the mountain tops to the valley floors, to the deep woods and the cascading rivers. A guide can describe a rocky overlook at such and so, but it cannot tell whether it's fogged in or not.

And who's to say whether we find in the fog the mystery of the north woods, or whether we find disappointment in not seeing farther?

I'd like to pick a defining experience, a place and time on the trail where it all came together for me in some kind of mystical peak experience. The retelling of this, I believe, could show the true value of the trail. But would it really? We can wax poetically all we want about the North Shore and the ridgeline, and it will all be true. The truth is, the value we experience depends on what we're seeking.

Instead, for me, faces come to mind. It is the faces and personalities of all those who brought the trail to life with sweat and good humor. It is Mark, Duane, Bob, Cory, Toivo, Neil, Harry, Stormy, and forty others who did the actual work of trail building. It is John, Tom, Bill, and Anne who, by the force of their character, willed the trail into existence.

For this trail to be really worthwhile, it should be more than just fun. It should heighten our awareness and appreciation of all that is natural. It should make us realize our place in the diverse complex web that is the land. With a little luck and a little help it might, for a few of us. And that would be worthwhile.

— TOM PETERSON

Acknowledgements

Many thanks to all who helped make this book happen.

Original Guide Editor: Andrew Slade

Photography: Jay Steinke, cover photo and Sam Cook, title page photo.

Project Coordinator: Nancy Hylden (1993 edition), Nancy Odden (1998 and 2001 editions), Gayle Coyer (2004 edition).

Trail Correspondents: Bill Anderson, Jill Dalbacka, Ron Wolff, Bunter Knowles, Don Schlossnagle, Jim Erickson, Ann Russ, Andrew Slade, Ruth Hiland, Karen Hanson, Miriam Graff, Bob Kotz, Bob Fox, Scott Beattie, Rudi Hargesheimer, Heidi Rigelman, John Green, Bill Dryborough, Ken Oelkers, Nancy Odden, Yafa Napadensky, and Joe Panci.

Field Checkers: Mike Anderson, Jim Erickson, Dave Geist, Rudi Hargesheimer, John Kohlstedt, Dick McDermott, Heidi Rigelman, Dick and Ella Slade, Anne and Peter Heegaard, Marilyn Vig, Andrew Slade, Bill Dryborough, Ted Tonkinson, Nancy Odden, Ken Oelkers, Gayle Coyer, and Joe Panci.

Contributing Writers: Deb Shubat, Nancy Hylden, John Green, Lee Radzak, Andrew Slade, Dave Schimpf, Rudi Hargesheimer, Catherine Long, John Kohlstedt, Jeanne Daniels, Anne McKinsey, Cindy Johnson-Groh, Janet Green, and Tricia Ryan.

Book Design and Layout: Sally Rauschenfels

Maps: Matt Kania.

GPS Data: Jeremy Ridlbauer. The project to GPS the trail was funded under the Coastal Zone Management Act, by NOAA's Office of Ocean and Coastal Resource Management, in conjunction with Minnesota's Lake Superior Coastal Program.

Book Production and Proofreading: Catherine Long, Tricia Ryan, Judy Gibbs, Kevin Roalson, Anne McKinsey, Rudi Hargesheimer, Tom Peterson, Kathy Hermes, Nancy Hylden, Jack Morris, Mark Wester, Sally Rauschenfels, Nancy Odden, Ann Possis, Ruth Hiland and Bill Dryborough.

Additional Thanks to Tom Peterson and Mark Wester for being the original Trail Coordinators.

Join the Superior Hiking Trail Association!

APPLICATION FOR MEMBERSHIP OR RENEWAL
(Note: Memberships run for one year from receipt of application)

Membership Categories:
(Check type of membership desired)

❑ Student ....$15   ❑ Individual $25
❑ Family 35   ❑ Youth organization/
❑ Supporting 100   Non-profit 40
❑ Life Member 500   ❑ Donation$_____

BUSINESS/CORPORATE

❑ Contributing ......$100   ❑ Sustaining $500
❑ Supporting.........250   ❑ Patron 1,000
❑ Donation $_____

Enclosed is $ _____ *for (check below):*
❑ **New membership**
❑ **Renewal   (Member number**_____**)**

Name: _____

Address: _____

_____

Home Tel: _____ Work Tel: _____

The Superior Hiking Trail Association is composed of volunteers.
To accomplish our goals, we need the active involvement of our members.

I am interested in helping the Superior Hiking Trail Association through:

❑ Constructing trails   ❑ Maintaining trails
❑ Fund-raising   ❑ Promotion/Publicity/Marketing
❑ Programs (leading hikes)   ❑ Art/Photography
❑ Group presentations
❑ Special skills:_____
❑ Liaison with other organizations_____
     (name of group)

MAIL TO Superior Hiking Trail Assn., PO Box 4, Two Harbors, MN 55616